ENTER THE DRAGON
DRAGON

THE 50TH ANNIVERSARY COMPANION

COMPILED AND EDITED BY

CARL FOX

WITH

ANDREW STATON

CONTRIBUTORS

**CARL FOX
ANDREW STATON
CHRIS KENT
PETER JAGGER**

BARNSLEY

Published by
PIT WHEEL PRESS LIMITED
www.pitwheelpress.com

**ENTER THE DRAGON
THE 50TH ANNIVERSARY COMPANION**

Copyright © 2024 Pit Wheel Press Limited.
All Right Reserved. No part of this book may be reproduced, scanned or distributed in any printed or electronic form without permission.

Standard Edition
First Edition 2024

Printed in the United Kingdom
ISBN 978-1-915414-20-5

*BRUCE LEE is a trademark of Bruce Lee Enterprises, LLC.
ENTER THE DRAGON is a trademark of Warner Bros.*

This publication is not affiliated with nor endorsed by Warner Bros. or their associates.

If the authors/compilers have inadvertently overlooked copyright holders connected with material within, please contact the publishers so that the situation can be rectified in future print editions.

ENTER THE DRAGON

THE 50TH ANNIVERSARY COMPANION

CONTENTS

ENTER THE DRAGON: EDITOR'S INTRODUCTION	11
ENTER THE DRAGON: 50TH ANNIVERSARY COMPANION	13
ENTER THE DRAGON: A SYNOPSIS	17
ENTER THE DRAGON: A HISTORY	21
ENTER THE DRAGON: BROUGHT TO BOOK	27
"YOU WANT TO BET?" JOHN SAXON IS ROPER IN ENTER THE DRAGON	31
AN INTERVIEW WITH ENTER THE DRAGON'S JOHN SAXON	35
JOHN SAXON: THE UNSEEN ROPER	45
SHIH KIEN: A TRIBUTE TO MR HAN	53
JIM KELLY: HIS THOUGHTS ON BRUCE LEE, ENTER THE DRAGON AND HIS FILM CAREER	57
BOB WALL: THE MAN WHO WHO WAS OHARRA	69
BOLO YEUNG: THE CHINESE HERCULES	79
ANGELA MAO YING: THE FIRST LADY OF KUNG FU	91
SAMMO HUNG: THE DYNAMIC MAESTRO	103
AHNA CAPRI: THE MADAM OF HAN'S ISLAND	107
AHNA CAPRI: THE 8MM FILM FOOTAGE	112
PETER ARCHER: FIGHTING WITHOUT FIGHTING	123
GEOFFREY WEEKS: THE CHIEF OF MI6	129
BETTY CHUNG: THE FEMALE SECRET AGENT	135
ROY CHIAO: THE SHAOLIN ABBOTT	143
TONY LIU: ROPER'S OPPONENT	147
PAT JOHNSON: IT'S THE DOUGH, ROPER!	153
YUEN WAH: THE MAN WHO MADE BRUCE LEE LOOK AMAZING	157
ROBERT CLOUSE: THE DIRECTOR OF ENTER THE DRAGON	177
FRED WEINTRAUB: PRODUCER OF ENTER THE DRAGON	189
PAUL HELLER: PRODUCER OF ENTER THE DRAGON	191
RAYMOND CHOW: THE MAN WHO HELPED CREATE A DRAGON	197
ANDRE MORGAN: ASSOCIATE PRODUCER	215
MICHAEL ALLIN: ENTER THE DRAGON SCRIPTWRITER	219
GIL HUBBS: CINEMATOGRAPHER OF ENTER THE DRAGON	223
LALO SCHIFRIN: THE MUSIC OF ENTER THE DRAGON	235
DAVE FRIEDMAN: STILLS PHOTOGRAPHER	243
ENTER THE DRAGON: A CULTURAL EVENT	247
WHEN BRUCE MET JACKIE AND WHAT HAPPENED NEXT!	259
ENTER THE DRAGON AND THE SAVAGERY OF THE BRITISH CENSORS	267
ENTER THE DRAGON: AN IN-DEPTH LOOK AT BRITISH CENSORSHIP	273
ENTER THE DRAGON: THE MISSING PIECES OF A CINEMATIC JIGSAW	291
ENTER THE DRAGON: THE GLOBAL IMPACT OF AN ICON	313
SELECTED FILMING LOCATIONS	327
ENTER THE DRAGON: CAST AND CREW	329
ENTER THE DRAGON @ 50: WRITING CREDITS	333
ENTER THE DRAGON @ 50: ABOUT THE CONTRIBUTORS	337

Motorcycle courier sent to deliver tournament invitations. It was felt that the scene slowed the film down, so the scene was dropped. A very short clip was used in the film's opening titles sequence.

ENTER THE DRAGON
EDITOR'S INTRODUCTION

Enter the Dragon will always be a special film to me; it was the very first Bruce Lee film I ever saw as a kid.

Someone once said that the most inspiring aspect about Bruce Lee was not his martial arts, his movies or his philosophy but his ability to inspire you to do something that you wouldn't ordinarily do. And that was true, for me, anyway.

It was through an appreciation of Bruce Lee that I started training in martial arts and began writing. For someone not very sports-inclined during high school, nor particularly gifted at English, I found a love for alternatives later on.

Andrew Staton, a friend of over twenty years, suggested a book to me about *Enter the Dragon* in late 2022 to celebrate the film's 50th anniversary in 2023. When Warner Bros announced their *Enter the Dragon* 4K UHD Blu-ray in early to mid 2023 without any new content, I decided to do a smaller companion book to accompany the new 4K UHD Blu-ray rather than a larger format book that everyone seemed to be doing.

The project turned out to be bigger than I could ever have imagined; the text files I had to work with were in a terrible state and most of them required at least a partial rewrite. The photos also required adjustment in places and some were totally unusable for print so alternatives had to be sourced. Some elements of the book were also redesigned halfway though to enable it to flow a little better in places. The planned 70 pages grew to 340 pages in the final draft.

I hope you enjoy the book and find it informative as we celebrate fifty years of quite possibly the finest martial arts film ever made - *Enter the Dragon*.

Carl Fox
Editor and Designer
July 2023

VICKERS
BRUCE LEE
JOHN SAXON - JIM KELLY
ENTER THE
DRAGON
COLOR UN-CUT
SEATS
RESTAURANT

ENTER THE DRAGON
THE 50TH ANNIVERSARY COMPANION

When *Enter the Dragon* was released in 1974 in the United Kingdom, it brought martial arts cinema to mainstream film viewers. Bruce Lee's physical prowess and unforgettable charm made him a cultural icon worldwide, and spearheaded the rise of the genre from the relative obscurity of Asian subculture, to the multi-billion-dollar pop-culture industry we have today. This was the first Hong Kong action picture to be produced by an American film company, and an early example of Hollywood's recognition of the importance of Asian Cinema. This movie has a lot to offer, a spy thriller set against the backdrop of a fighting tournament on a secret island owned by a reclusive criminal mastermind with a removable hand, this is a bit of Hong Kong James Bond, combining action, humour, drama, and jump-kicks. With crossover performances by actor John Saxon, and Karate Champion Jim Kelly, and punctuated by Lee's indomi-

table personality, *Enter the Dragon* stands out as a benchmark of cinematic history. But the film fell foul of the British Board of Film Censors' (BBFC) anxieties about violence and martial arts weaponry. After reading in Time Out magazine about the ready availability of flying stars and rice flails (nunchaku), chief censor James Ferman effectively banned such instruments from UK screens until the turn of the century, arguing that – unlike guns – these weapons could be legally purchased in the UK. Thankfully today, the totally uncensored film stands as testament to Lee's extraordinary star power, and the balletic skill of his physical feats. As we celebrate the release of The Bruce Lee Master 4K Blu-ray 4K Remaster from Warner Brothers, it may be the last time this film will ever be released in this media format or any other format and only be available on Video on Demand.

For this reason, we would love to dedicate this 50th Anniversary Special to the loyal Bruce Lee Fans around the world.

So to you all remember:-

"It is like a finger pointing to the moon; do not concentrate on the finger or you will miss all the heavenly glory."

Andrew Staton
Contributing Editor
July 2023

ENTER THE DRAGON
A SYNOPSIS

Enter the Dragon takes Bruce Lee into the island fortress of a warlord of crime, Han, who carries on his opium smuggling and prostitution activities under the disguise of a martial arts academy. Determined to avenge the death of his sister, Lee penetrates Han's stronghold and enters the brutal martial arts tournament Han is staging.

Then follows a visual feast of spectacular martial arts matches that combine skills in Karate, Judo, Taekwondo, Tai Chi Chuan, and Hapkido. Bruce Lee staged these fighting sequences himself, demonstrating experienced awareness of film rhythm and dramatic timing as well as mastery of the martial arts that made him famous.

Joining Lee in *Enter the Dragon* is John Saxon as Roper, on the run from the Mafia due to his gambling debts and whose fine martial arts technique comes from long study of Karate and Tai Chi Chuan. The film also introduces Jim Kelly, the 1971 International Middleweight Karate Champion as Williams. Other outstanding martial art specialists whose talents lend realism to *Enter the Dragon* include Bob Wall, the 1970 United States Professional Karate Champion; Peter Archer, the 1971 Commonwealth Karate Champion; Yang Sze, the Shotokan Champion of Southeast Asia, and Angela Mao Ying, the Black Belt Hapkido Champion of Okinawa.

Bruce Lee's own performance, as actor and fighter, demonstrates all the qualities that have kept his reputation alive since his untimely death at the age of 32 on the 20th July 1973.

In action, he moves with the speed and confidence of a cat swatting at string. Even in repose, his understated presence is magnetic. The martial arts enthusiasm he helped inspire still continues, and crowds still gather wherever his films are shown.

Enter the Dragon is widely regarded as one of the greatest martial arts films of all time. In 2004, it was selected for preservation in the United States National Film Registry by the Library of Congress as being "culturally, historically, or aesthetically significant". Among the first films to combine martial arts action with spy film elements and the emerging blaxploitation genre, its success led to a series of similar productions combining the martial arts and blaxploitation genres. Its themes generated scholarly debate about the changes taking place within post-colonial Asian societies following the end of World War II.

Enter the Dragon is also considered one of the most influential action films of all time, with its success contributing to mainstream worldwide interest in the martial arts as well as inspiring numerous fictional works, including action films, television shows, action games, comic books, manga and anime.

Sammo Hung squares off against Bruce Lee in the opening sequence of *Enter the Dragon*.

BRUCE LEE & ENTER THE DRAGON

Enter the Dragon was the movie that made martial arts films popular in the west. It was not the first to be seen in Britain; this privilege went to the Shaw Brothers movie *King Boxer* (aka *Five Fingers Of Death* in The US) starring Lo Lieh, Tien Feng (*Fist of Fury*), and Yang Sze (*Enter the Dragon*). It was released mid-1973 and got the British movie going public geared up for the Kung Fu Movie Craze that was to follow the next year. The craze was helped on by the Warner Brothers TV show *Kung Fu* starring David Carradine, which would be revealed years later to be based on *The Warrior*, an unmade television series devised by Lee. Ditched by Warner Brothers for the lead role because he was 'too Chinese', it was thought that western audiences would not accept Lee in a lead role; an action which showed the racism prevalent in Hollywood at the time.

On 13th January 1974, *Enter the Dragon* was released in London's Leicester Square before enjoying a nationwide release all over the UK. Bruce Lee's fourth movie took Britain by storm and martial arts clubs were set up all over the country - overnight in some cases - to profiteer from the demand by the public to learn martial arts, especially Kung Fu.

Enter the Dragon was sadly Bruce's final movie and was the only one he made in English, with an American cast and crew. Although it had Hollywood money, it still remained very much a Hong Kong movie, with the whole thing being filmed in Hong Kong and using the Golden Harvest studios with owner Raymond Chow serving as co-producer. It is very much a Western take on the Kung Fu movie, which was then a genre in its infancy. Lee had only been a movie star for two years, and made only three full movies as an adult prior to beginning work on *Enter the Dragon*.

Looking back at the production of the movie, it really does qualify as a fascinating experiment; an attempt to see wheth-

er this new foreign subgenre would work in a more American context. Even though the movie was, in a lot of ways, a glorious mess, it turned out to be a huge success on just about every level of film-making.

Lee wasn't exactly the main drive behind *Enter the Dragon* in the same way he was with his beloved *Way Of The Dragon*, the movie he made some months before. Warner Brothers played cautious in all aspects of the movie and gave the director's chair to Robert Clouse, who had only made a few movies previous to this and who would never make anything anywhere near this iconic after but every one he did make afterwards, it had the stamp of "From the Director of *Enter the Dragon*", on it.

Lee was the primary creative force behind the movie, and although some said he was difficult to get on set, he really did co-write the script, put together its great action scenes, and made sure to put his personality in there whenever possible. Early in the movie, there's a deeply Chinese philosophical scene in which Lee is talking to a young student, insists that the kid put, "emotional content and not anger". Lee then spends the rest of the movie showing us what a kick with real emotional content looks like.

The whole movie is designed as a vehicle for Lee to show his art, skill and charisma. He included more philosophy than was in the script, when he demonstrates "the art of fighting without fighting." He gets all the best scenes and coolest moments. His character name in the film is "Lee," and it feels less like a character and more like the man himself. Lee, of course, understood what he'd need to do in a movie for American audiences. He'd lived much of his life in the US, played Kato on the American TV show *The Green Hornet*, and played other small roles in a few other American TV shows as well as *Marlowe*, a movie starring James Garner. He knew what he was doing and with American production values, as well as a great music score from the great Lalo Schifrin (*Mission Impossible* theme and soundtracks to Clint Eastwood's *Dirty Harry* series of movies), Lee ended up looking cooler than he ever had before.

Even though Lee dominates the movie, there is some typical American-studio stereotyping in there. For example, the bad guy, Han, is practically a parody of the scheming Bond villain; he pets a fluffy cat and says things like, "We are investing in corruption." And the movie dedicates a baffling portion of its running time to two heroes who are pointedly not Bruce Lee.

Luckily those two heroes were excellent; John Saxon, who would later go on to star in Wes Craven acclaimed horror movie *A Nightmare On Elm Street* as lead character Nancy's Police Chief father.

Saxon was great portraying a gambling-addicted international-playboy type, and his screen-fighting was better than an-

The evil Han, played by Shih Kien.

yone could have reasonably expected.

Karate champion, Jim Kelly, who had only been in one movie previous called *Melinda* (1972) was a total find but had not been the first choice for the role. He replaced Rockne Tarkington, who quit the film three days before production was due to start because he thought the pay was too low.

Kelly's character was a black-power archetype - not really a character at all - but he had the charisma to carry it off. Kelly's screen-fighting was very impressive, as you would expect considering he had won the World Middleweight Karate title at the Long Beach Championships in 1971.

Still, Saxon and Kelly were no match for Lee, in terms of screen presence or screen-fighting ability When we get to see Lee at work, he's at his absolute peak, taking out hordes of henchmen in an underground lair or fighting them in a martial arts courtyard. The final fight scene, in which he takes on Hong Kong movie veteran Shih Kien, is a visual feast. The Hall of Mirrors effects against Kien's deadly bladed-hand is magnificent but Lee's best fight is probably the brutal destruction of Han's American bodyguard, Oharra, played by world Karate Champion Bob Wall.

There is plenty of photographic evidence that Lee was involved in every aspect of this movie's production especially the

fight scenes, and in that cavern fight, he even kills off a very young Jackie Chan, who we all know has gone on to greater things.

All in all, Bruce Lee's wiry physique, strong presence, and fantastic martial arts action have assured *Enter the Dragon* a solid place in the hearts of action fans of all ages, and Lee's long, final duel with Han is a classic.

Although to a computer game addicted generation that play advanced martial arts games on their games consoles on a daily basis, in some way, that makes the film a little dated. There is something so straightforward about how *Enter the Dragon* delivers the goods that earned it respect from the western film critics and it remains an iconic must-watch for all ages as the ultimate martial arts movie, even today. Sadly, we'll never know how many more martial arts movies would have been made had Lee survived. But at least he left us with this ground-breaking movie that has influenced every martial arts film and television show that has been made since its release in 1974. For this, we honour, respect, celebrate and remember the world's greatest martial arts hero of all time - Bruce Lee.

Enter the Dragon

Kung Fu Killers on the loose —
now an action-packed film starring Bruce

ENTER THE DRAGON
BROUGHT TO BOOK

In 1973 in the U.S and 1974 in the United Kingdom, *Enter the Dragon* became the ultimate Martial Arts movie and started a genre in the west and pushed people into practising Asian martial Arts. The script was written in the style of a James Bond film, right down to the villain having a white Persian cat like Blofeld in the 007 movies.

However back in the early seventies there was little chance of being able to see the film again unless it was shown at the cinema again as a double bill which did happen quite a few times, with the likes of *Freebie and the Bean*, *Death Race 2000* and the Bruceploitation movie *The Dragon Lives*. These were the days before VHS existed, and the only other way was to buy a costly 8mm film projector and purchase an even more expensive cut down version of the film

So, at that time the only other way to recreate the magic of *Enter the Dragon* was buy buying the paperback book by Mike Roote. The movie tie-in novel was released a few weeks before the movie in the UK on 1st January 1974 and was an instant bestseller. The American publishers, Award Books, had the great tag line on the cover "Kung Fu Killers on the Loose - A dynamite novel by Mike Roote. Now an action-packed movie. Original screenplay by Michael Allin." On the back, the text was just as wild, as it boasted, "Their Deadly Mission to Crack the Forbidden Fortress of Han. The ultimate martial arts masterpiece lavishly filmed by Warner Bros, in Hong Kong and the China Sea. Now an explosive novel."

The British publishers, Tandem, were a little more reserved with the tag lines on the cover, so although it did state on the cover "Kung Fu Killers on the loose," it alternatively said, "Now an action-packed film starring Bruce Lee."

The novelisation stays reasonably close to the film with just a few variations. The book opens with Roper and Williams fleeing the US whereas these scenes appear as much later flashbacks in the film. However, Braithwaite arrives at the Shaolin Temple first by limousine and enters through large temple doors, after crossing a courtyard. Here he sees two men in black Kung Fu suits preparing to do battle, Braithwaite is treated to a spectacular Kung Fu fight sequence and is amazed at the skill and talent of the two combatants. When the fight finishes, the victor is a young man (Lee) who walks past Braithwaite and goes through into an inner temple to talk to the monk who is the high priest. The conversation between the two of them is in the restored 25th anniversary print of the movie.

Also, in the book, the secret intelligence agency Lee is working for is called F.A.D.E., which is never used in the film. Some of the characters that appear in the film are described differently to how they look on screen; for instance, Bolo is Turkish, not Chinese and some scenes are more elaborately staged in the book, such as a long sequence inside the Shaolin Temple that, in the film, is just shot in a garden. There's more of a backstory regarding Han's sex trafficking of women.

By reading the book, you can almost tell that Roote is writing the novel without ever seeing Bruce 's fight scenes, so is unaware of which moves or weapons are used and where. There are terrific martial arts descriptive lines like "Launching himself high in the air with a leaping kick, Lee came down like a rocket, legs and fists of steel flying" once every few pages but there's no descriptive Kung Fu moves anywhere. The book also shows that it was written before the film was completed as the legendary Hall of Mirrors fight is not even in it.

A little-known fact about the novelisation is that there is no one called, 'Mike Roote.' It turns out to be a pseudonym of Leonore Fleischer, who was an American writer specialising in novelisations of movies. She published over forty novelisations under her own name and a variety of pseudonyms.

In 1969, Fleischer, then a senior editor at Ballantine Books, was invited to write a novelisation of biker film *C.C. & Company*. She accepted due to financial difficulties caused by her recent divorce, and published the book under the pseudonym Mike Roote, concerned that publishing under her own name would cause problems with her employers. Fleischer went on to publish six novelizations under the name Roote, including the bestselling novelization of *Enter the Dragon* (1974). The others were *Born To Win* (1970), *Scorpio* (1972), *Prime Cut* (1972) and *Badge 373* (1973).

She published a further six under the name Alexander Edwards, as well as several under other pseudonyms, only publishing under her own name once she left her job and began to write freelance full-time.

Believe it or not but *Enter the Dragon*, was written in a weekend on a speed binge, like all her early novels. "I would sit down on Friday night and take amphetamines," explained Fleischer. "On Monday morning I would topple over sideways with a completed manuscript." A few years later, she gave up the amphetamines and claimed the secret of still producing so many books was getting up early, going to bed early, and not having sex.

By reading *Enter the Dragon*, you may be forgiven for thinking 'Mike Roote' was the kind of cigar smoking whisky drinking journalist as this is what 'his' writing suggests, *Enter the Dragon* wouldn't be more than a mildly entertaining read. However, now knowing it was penned by Leonore Fleischer, The feels that touch more enjoyable. You can see she was gleefully experimenting with her writing and taking on the task of writing about Kung Fu, which was a subject she and the west had little knowledge about in the early 70's, and having little resemblance to the real thing, it makes the content a little more fun to read.

The best example of this is on the very last page. They say write what you know and you can imagine this is exactly how Fleischer felt, hitting the deadline on that book after her two-day speed binge: "Like a knight of the Middle Ages, Roper sat resting on his sword, his chin supported by the upturned hilt. His face was wet with blood and sweat but he was grinning in satisfaction. It had been a good job well done."

Somehow if she had seen the film, you can rest assured that the ending of the book would have lain at the feet of the man who put the magic in the movie - the one and only Bruce Lee.

JOHN SAXON
"YOU WANT TO BET?"

John Saxon was born Carmine Orrico on August 5, 1936, in Brooklyn, New York, the first child of Antonio and Ann Orrico. His mother was born in Caserta, a small city near Naples, Italy.

John became interested in acting as a teenager and began attending dramatic school in Manhattan while still going to New Utrecht High School in Brooklyn. A photograph - the result of a photo illustration job brought him to the attention of a Hollywood agent who recommended that he come to Los Angeles to start his career. Three weeks after his arrival, at the grand old age of seventeen, John Saxon auditioned for, and won a Stock Contract at Universal Studios.

The next couple of years, studying at the studio's acting school, were anxious and difficult, until roles came to prove to himself and others what he could do.

After much screen-testing, Saxon won a co-starring role with Esther Williams in the 1956 drama, *The Unguarded Moment*. A series of young leading-man roles followed during the 1950's: *Rock Pretty Baby*, *Summer Love*, *The Restless Years*, *The Reluctant Debutante* with Sandra Dee and *This Happy Feeling* with Debbie Reynolds.

By 1958, John was a highly publicised teenage heartthrob in movie magazines and by the late 1950's he began to explore an inclination toward character roles in the theatre, films, and in many of the first feature length films made for television.

By 1960, however, John was doing character roles, to explore his talent as an actor, in such films as *Cry Tough*, *The Big Fisherman*, *The Unforgiven*, *The Plunderers* and *Warhunt*.

In 1961, his contract with Universal Studios ended and he went to Italy to promote a European acting career. After a year, he returned to Los Angeles, concentrating on character acting in scores of television shows.

John Saxon as Lt. Thompson in *A Nightmare on Elm Street*.

In 1965 John won the role of Chuy Medina, a Mexican bandit, playing opposite Marlon Brando in *The Appaloosa*. John succeeded in winning good reviews and much attention for this portrayal.

A new contract with Universal led John to appear in many of the earliest feature length films made expressly for television, such as *Doomsday Flight*, *Winchester 73* and *The Bold Ones* TV series.

In 1973 John co-starred in *Enter the Dragon* with Bruce Lee, a film that has achieved cult classic status and in the 1980's John was a regular on *Falcon Crest*.

John Saxon has appeared in more than 100 feature films including *Posse from Hell*, *Joe Kidd*, *Black Christmas*, *Fast Company*, *The Electric Horseman*, *Blood Beach*, *The Battle Beyond the Stars*, *Wrong is Right*, *A Nightmare on Elm Street*, *Beverly Hills Cop 3*, *Dusk Till Dawn*, *Lady Luck*, *The Player* and *Outta Time*.

His many television appearances include *Murder, She Wrote*, episodes of Melrose Place and most recently, the *CSI: Crime Scene Investigation* special, *Grave Danger*, directed by Quentin Tarantino.

In later years, he was busy with features in the US and abroad. As well as many television appearances, he also appeared on stage with Debbie Reynolds in *Love Letters*.

During his off-screen time, John wrote several screenplays,

Bruce Lee demonstrates to John Saxon how he should throw a punch at Yang Sze (off camera).

which he hoped to direct one day, but his death on 25th July 2020 put an end to those plans. In a fitting finale, he is buried near his old *Enter the Dragon* co-star Bruce Lee in Seattle's Lakeview cemetery.

AN INTERVIEW WITH
JOHN SAXON

The following interview was conducted on the 17th May 2002 at the autograph collector's show Autographica in Northampton, England.

What attracted you to the role of Roper in Enter the Dragon?

Well it wasn't actually the role that attracted me to the project so much as the feeling of the martial arts, which I had been somewhat connected to over a number of years on and off. I felt that by the time the script came to me, I sensed a spreading awareness, a spreading interest in the subject and I had thought then, along with the fact that I had heard of Bruce Lee and had seen him here and there, though I had not met him. I thought that the project would have some appeal, probably large appeal. It had greater appeal than I had expected but I thought it was going to be, the time had come, that the public would be interested in this.

How much martial arts experience did you have prior to filming Enter the Dragon?

Well, I started doing some Judo back in 1958 for a brief while. Then in the early 60s, I began studying Shotokan Karate and I did that for about four years until about 1968 when I was very, very busy filming here and there in Europe and America. Then I became interested in Tai Chi Chuan and stuff because I was getting older and I had a family, so that was my background. I had some experience.

Did you learn anything from Bruce Lee on the set?

Yes, we spoke constantly about martial arts. We got along very well and I was interested that this project kind of reinvigorated some interest that I had, that had diminished. So

THE 50TH ANNIVERSARY COMPANION

John Saxon in one of his many discussions with Bruce Lee on the set of *Enter the Dragon*.

Bruce Lee choreographs a fight scene between co-stars John Saxon and Yang Sze.

I was willing and interested in all of his ideas. We would talk about martial arts things constantly. I had already begun to be interested in what they call the softer Chinese martial arts like Tai Chi and stuff of that nature, plus other things I had heard about that I had never really seen such as Pak Gua. Bruce was very interested, in a respect that he kind of thought that most of these things were a head trip; not very realistic. He presented himself in the movies as a Chinese martial artist but in fact he was very eclectic. He had put together everything that he had ever observed or had been interested in, for his own use.

Were you witness to any of the challenges made to Bruce on the set of Enter the Dragon?

There was one incident which really doesn't require a great deal of conversation. It was just a personal challenge. It occurred between an extra and Bruce. It was in Cantonese so I don't know what the words were but I think the intent was clear. What the extra was saying was, "You're just a movie actor. You're not for real," or something like that, and there were a whole bunch of extras around listening to this so it was obviously a verbal challenge Bruce felt he had to deal with. Bruce said, "Well, alright, come on down and show me what you're going to do." Bruce just quickly smacked him across the side of the face and the kid got a bloody nose. He put his hands up and that was it.

Were there any problems that the cast and crew encountered while filming, in terms of language?

Yes. This was a production that had an American crew of three maybe four - the cameraman, the actors, the director and the producers - maybe half a dozen and there was one intermediary. I think his name was Chaplin Chang. He spoke English and he spoke Cantonese and I think Mandarin too. So he was the interpreter and a lot of things didn't get interpreted properly. Things that were intended to be built for the set, that were models, came as models. And we were, "No, we meant for real!" Things of this nature, just got lost in translation, and they were funny.

Did Bruce ever act as a mediator between the Chinese and American crew?

John Saxon in discussion with Bruce Lee during time off on the set of *Enter the Dragon*.

Were you aware that actress Ahna Capri was shooting some Super 8 footage on the set?

Later. I think I met her somewhere and she said that she had this footage, and she asked me what she should do with it. I don't know what became of it and I don't think I've seen it.

There were rumoured to be many hours of footage shot on the set that were to be made into a documentary. Do you recall that footage being shot?

Not really. I don't know what was intended for documentary

purposes. When you ask that question, what really comes to my mind is that, at a certain point, after I had decided that this was a project that was going to work very well or that it was going to have an audience appeal, I re-read the script, and I wasn't confident that it wasn't an acting role enough for me because as a script, it was more of a treatment. It was about 45 pages or something like that and everything was sketched in and I began to have second thoughts and I called the producers and I said, "I think you guys could just get a stunt guy to do this role." "Why, why, what's wrong?" they said. So I said, "Well there's nothing wrong, I just think there's enough substance to act." They said, "Can we talk about it?" I told them that I didn't see anything to talk about. Finally I said, "Let's talk it over," and we did. Some scenes I suggested never made it onto the screen. Nevertheless, I am very pleased about having done the film.

What did you think of the quality of Bruce Lee's fight choreography in Enter the Dragon?

Obviously, it was very innovative and nobody had ever seen anything like that before. That's what made the film a success. This almost magical kind of fighting, fighting five or six people, on film it looked incredible, because of his prowess. I think he knew what he was doing. He had a background – his father was in the Chinese opera. Chinese opera, whether it is Peking or otherwise were highly martial

Bruce Lee and John Saxon await the call for "Action" on the tennis court location near the end of *Enter the Dragon*.

arts referenced - all of the stories have some aspects of martial arts. Most of the people who did it were capable of some kind of martial arts. They weren't fighters but they were great technicians. I realised that Bruce was influenced by that as well. On film, he made a very interesting distinction. He would say something about, "On film I do one thing, and in reality I do another," or something like that. Some of the things go back to the Chinese opera, especially with the music. They bring together sound with dynamic movements.

Did Bruce ever complain or mention anything to you about headaches on the set of the film?

Yes, but after the filming, not during filming. When I had finished, I left with my wife and son, and we went to Thailand and Japan, and then I came back home and they were continuing working on the last scene, that mirror scene. Sometime in May, I got a call at my home from Bruce and I said, "Gee, what are you doing here?" and he spoke in very grave terms. He said, "I've been fainting and maybe there won't be a Bruce Lee," and I was like, "What? What is he talking about? This is very unlike him to speak this way." So I kind of kidded him. But I got concerned because he wasn't somebody to talk like that. So I called him a few days later and he was in very high spirits. He told me that the doctor had told him that he had a body of an 18 year old, so we thought the matter was all over, and had been taken care of. Then, I think he died about a few weeks later. *Enter the Dragon* was made over 30 years ago and it is still remembered as probably the greatest martial arts film of all time.

I am astounded at the film's success. Young guys feel as if their life was changed when they saw the film and they went into the martial arts. I am a little perplexed by it. I've been asked about Bruce Lee so often that once I had a dream that it was night time and I was walking across a desolate parking lot and there was one street lamp in the background that was very dim, very foreboding and I walked to my car. I was just about to put my keys into my car and someone put a gun to my head and I looked up and the guy looked at me and said, "Man, you're John Saxon. What was it like working with Bruce Lee?

THE UNSEEN ROPER

Scripts go through many transformations before they go into production and even when being filmed, the script can change many times before the finished product is seen on the screen.

In speaking to John Saxon, it seems that the script used on the set of *Enter the Dragon* was one written by Michael Allin, but there is a script in the public domain, which John tells us, was written by Fred Weintraub and Paul Heller, two of the producers on *Enter the Dragon*. It was difficult to assess which script this was and John couldn't even tell us if some of the changes in the script were changes he had asked for or not. They weren't in the final cut because Fred Weintraub told him, "they had been lost in a lab".

His main interest in this script was to see if himself or Jim Kelly was the one to die in the movie. He had heard a rumour about a year before that Jim Kelly had been told that Roper was supposed to be the one to die instead of Williams. The reason John thinks Weintraub said this was to keep Kelly on good terms with him as he had another film he wanted him to do.

Saxon's awareness to this fact could possibly have some substance as he remembered an instance near the very end of the shoot when Kelly told him, with a certain amount of emphasis that John couldn't understand at the time, that he "was never going to die again in a film." He thought it was an odd thing to say to him since he had never felt bad about dying in a film; in fact he has died or been killed in more than a dozen movies.

Taking a reflective look at this Weintraub and Heller script, we try to reveal some scenes that show The Unseen Roper.

The first differences of many in this script compared to the final shooting script is when Roper first meets Lee on the junk. There is a lot more dialogue between Lee, Roper and Williams and there seems to be a mix up on who says what, especially

when the boat is docking and we first meet Tania (Ahna Capri). In addition, Lee's lines are much longer and liberally scattered with Chinese philosophy.

The script forwards the idea that Roper has very early scenes with Tania as she introduces herself and sets up the later encounter which does occur in the film.

Later in the script, Roper labels Lee's character with the nickname he uses for the rest of the film, 'The Philosopher', because he spouts Chinese philosophy every time he meets him. This occurs when they make their second encounter at Han's banquet. Again in the script, there is some really interesting dialogue, which is not seen in the film, conducted between the Roper and Lee characters.

In this script, after Williams has been killed, Roper meets Han in a garden, not in Han's Palace, where a long scene takes place as Han explains to Roper that we wants him to join his team.

After the death of his friend Williams, this script describes a scene were Roper visits Tania for a third time in a very drunken state and forces himself upon her in an effort to deal with his personal loss of a friend.

The big, end fight scene in this script is very different to the one that was filmed. In brief, once Roper has chosen to side with Lee, he fights back to back with him then tells Lee that he especially wants to confront Bolo himself. But the outcome is

THE 50TH ANNIVERSARY COMPANION

A rehearsal between John Saxon and Anna Capri for the missing scene where a drunk Roper confronts Tania after learning of Williams' fate.

still the same as Roper champions Bolo.

With this celebrative brochure, it is hoped that a little more light has been shed on the Roper character and his relationship with the Lee character in this ultimate tribute to the greatest martial arts motion picture of all time, *Enter the Dragon*.

Bruce Lee and John Saxon in discussion during time off from filming *Enter the Dragon*.

Bruce Lee, Robert Clouse and John Saxon pose for a photograph during time off from filming *Enter the Dragon*.

SHIH KIEN
A TRIBUTE TO MR. HAN

Shih Kien was born in Hong Kong on 1st January 1913. His family came from Shigang Village, Panyu, Guangdong in the Republic of China.

Kien entered the film industry in 1939, where his first job was as a make-up man on a film, literally translated as, *The Peerless Beauty*. He made his debut as an actor the following year in *A Flower in the Storm*.

In his fifty-six years of active service in the Hong Kong film industry between 1939 and 1995, he worked continuously as an actor and sometimes, a martial arts instructor within the film industry.

Shih Kien came to his acting career with a background in martial arts, rather than the usual opera training. His first teacher seems to have been Chao Lien-cheng, a specialist in the Northern Shaolin style who was affiliated with the Chin Woo Association founded by Huo Yuan Jia (The legendary Kung Fu master, whose death is the main subject of Bruce Lee's *Fist of Fury*).

Shih eventually became a full time student at the Chin Woo branch in Canton (Guangzhou), where he trained with a well known master named Sun Yu-fung. Sun's expertise was in Do (broadsword or saber) and Lohan techniques. In later years, he described his personal style as Mi Tsong Lohan Chuan or 'Combined Lohan Fist.' He also studied Chinese wrestling, or Shuai Jiao, and Tan Tui (Spring Leg) kicking techniques. Other teachers included Chao Kuei-lin, who taught him Mantis style and Eagle Claw boxing, and Wong Yung-feng, who trained him in the use of an obscure 'secret weapon', called Piao, which seems to have been a kind of dart.

He finally received instructor certification in a number of styles, including Eagle Claw and Choy Lay Fut. Among his students was Lee Koon Hung, Grandmaster of Choy Lay Fut.

He became best known as a veteran actor of Cantonese movies and his name was to become synonymous with villains, as he tended to play evil characters. In Hong Kong, there is a slang expression that compares people's evil deeds with Shih Kien's, despite the fact these deeds were committed by the evil characters he played, not the actor. He was actually well-respected within the Hong Kong motion picture industry and recognised as a very kind and passionate man.

His eclectic background contributed to his success as a martial arts actor, since it gave him the versatility needed to master the choreography quickly. It makes sense that Lohan boxing became Shih's specialty, since it emphasises dramatic poses that mimic traditional Buddhist devotional statues - ideal training for an aspiring Kung Fu performer!

He played a villain of almost all the classics of the time, such as 1964's Ru Lai Shen Zhang and 1965's Liu Zhi Qin Mo and in the majority of films in the Huang Fei-Hong series. Although Shih picked up a couple of 'assistant action director' credits during his lengthy screen career, he doesn't seem to have been interested in controlling the entire choreography of a film. Probably he has always been one of the stalwart and easily overlooked pillars of the Hong Kong action film genre, ready to contribute ideas or bits of business, if needed, or even set his own moves, but he was also just as happy to take the

Bruce Lee and Shih Kien in discussion during time off from filming.

choreography and adapt it to his characterisation. He could do a fight scene in the soft opera style if he had to, but give him a chance to show real Kung Fu onscreen, and boy, he really stood out!

One of the first things that strike a modern viewer watching Shih's old fights on film is how lively he is. He bounds into the fray, jumps and skips, and tosses in a front jumping kick or spin without slowing down. That would be the Tan Tui influence. Even when forced to slow down or soften his onslaught to match his opponent, his movement is always very emotionally expressive. And that would be the Lohan influence showing up. His weapon strikes were precise and powerful. He was a true professional, a master of his trade.

He is best known to western audiences as the villainous Han in Bruce Lee's 1973 martial arts classic *Enter the Dragon*. It is no wonder that when Warner Brothers teamed up with Bruce Lee and the Golden Harvest studio to make this ground breaking action movie, Shih Kien was tapped to play the evil Mr. Han. He had the moves and the experience. Although he was nearly three decades older than Lee and had to be stunt-doubled in many shots, he still took an amazing amount of abuse from the younger fighter. His own performance emphasised raw power and physical tension rather than the fluidity he was capable of. Altogether he made a worthy adversary for Lee in the most famous martial arts film of all time.

Han (Shih Kien) on his outdoor throne with his female bodyguards.

ENTER THE DRAGON

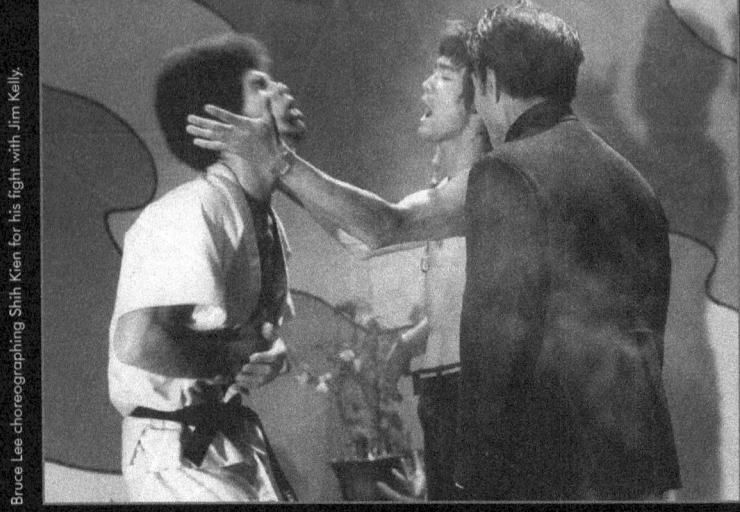

Bruce Lee choreographing Shih Kien for his fight with Jim Kelly.

He followed this success with such films like *The Private Eyes* (1977), directed by Michael Hui and *The System* (1979) directed by Peter Yung.

Later in his acting career, he took on a comedic role with Jackie Chan in *The Young Master* (1980). He also acted in dramatic roles in such non-wuxia films as *Hong Kong 1941*.

His earlier non-action roles included appearances in the Cantonese trilogy based on Ba Jin's novels *Family* (1953), *Spring* (1953) and *Autumn* (1954)

He also frequently appeared in local television series from 1967, making his first appearance in an episode of RTHK series *Below the Lion Rock*, there was no doubt that as he matured, he became an excellent character actor. Shih Kien retired from the entertainment industry in the mid-1990s.

His final film role was in Bosco Lam's comedy *Hong Kong Addams Family* (1994)

Shih Kien was rumoured to have died in 1999, but appeared in the 2003 documentary *Chop Socky: Cinema Hong Kong* at the age of 90. Then the actor was reportedly hospitalised in 2008 for piles but he recovered and appeared then to be fighting fit.

Then early reports on the morning of June 4, 2009 - the day of his passing - did not say what the cause of death was. Later it was revealed that he had died of kidney failure. At the

Han gives Roper a tour of his operations in *Enter the Dragon*.

time of his death, Kien was believed to be one of the oldest living actors in China.

Hong Kong had lost one of its greatest film treasures as Gregory So, Hong Kong's Secretary for Commerce and Economic Development expressed, "Mr. Shih's brilliant career in the performing arts industry started in the 1940s. Since then he devoted lifelong commitment to the industry. He played a villain role in the Wong Fei-hung film series and had become one of the most recognisable faces of Hong Kong cinema."

"With his death, Hong Kong has lost an outstanding performing arts talent. On behalf of the Commerce and Economic Development Bureau, I offer our deepest condolences to Mr. Shih's family."

Over his long prestigious career, he received several Hong Kong Film Awards, including a Professional Spirit Award, a 1996 and 2003 Lifetime Achievement Award and Golden Bauhinia Award.

JIM KELLY
HIS THOUGHTS ON BRUCE LEE, ENTER THE DRAGON AND HIS FILM CAREER

Jim Kelly was a martial artist and all round athlete who is best-known for co-starring with John Saxon in the Bruce Lee movie *Enter the Dragon*. With his signature Afro hairstyle, athletic build, top-notch Karate skills and so-cool-he's-hot charisma, Jim Kelly was one of the top martial arts film stars of the 1970s. He put his skills to use in what have been coined as "Blaxploitation" films of the era, including *Three the Hard Way*, *Golden Needles* and *Black Belt Jones*; the latter being perhaps the only film in cinema history to feature a fight finale in a soap-filled car wash! But what was Kelly's thoughts on Bruce Lee, *Enter the Dragon* and his short-lived movie career? Here is what he said:

> Once I got the part of Williams I was sent to Hong Kong for two months and that was an experience not only was Hong Kong an experience but it was an incredible experience working with Bruce Lee. I was not supposed to be killed in that movie; John Saxon was supposed to be killed and at that time, that was my second film and John Saxon had made twenty-four movies - or something like that anyway. His agent said, "If you want John Saxon for the film, Jim will have to get killed, not John." I was happy to do it as this was only my second film to my credit and the film gave me a lot of exposure all over the world and opened incredible doors for me as far as getting me known in the film business.
>
> I loved working with John Saxon and it was a great honour to work with the greatest martial artist who ever lived, Bruce Lee. In my time in Karate competitions, I fought the best, I trained

with the best, so I know great martial artists, but there has never been and never will be anybody like Bruce Lee. He was unbelievable, absolutely unbelievable. You will never know how great this guy was; a martial arts guy who knew his stuff. I have stories on Bruce Lee I do not share with anyone because I know and respect the people it concerns, and it is not necessary for me to name names. I know who Bruce Lee sparred with, but Bruce Lee was untouchable. The speed and the timing that Bruce had was unbelievable. Bruce was the type of guy that would spar with you and it did not matter what size the guy was - Lightweight, Middleweight, Heavyweight - he would spar with you. Hands and feet first and then he would say, "Let's just spar with our hands," and he would still win. All this rubbish that Bruce was not a real fighter is just that; if he had wanted to fight in Point-Karate, he would have made the adjustment if he needed to. Some of his students were World Champion Points-Karate fighters and even though they trained with him, when it came to Points-Karate, they made the adjustment, and whatever style or combative method you used, Bruce would have made the adjustment to win the fight. Bruce Lee was absolutely unbelievable; so many people have asked me how great Bruce Lee was and I say, "Bruce Lee was a step above everybody."

Fred Weintraub asked me if I liked the film business. I said, "It's great," and when I got back to Los Angeles, my agent said, "Jim, you have got to go to Warner Brothers because they want to talk to you about something." So I said, "OK." Warners wanted to talk to me about a three-picture deal

Bruce Lee choreographing Jim Kelly on the tennis courts of Enter the Dragon as Lee's butler, Wo Ngan, looks on.

Jim Kelly blocks Bruce Lee's kick while choreographing his fight scene for *Enter the Dragon*.

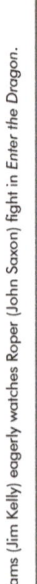
Williams (Jim Kelly) eagerly watches Roper (John Saxon) fight in *Enter the Dragon*.

plus an option on a TV series. Black Belt Jones *was the first one,* Golden Needles *the second one and* Hot Potato *the third one. I loved working with Gloria Hendry in* Black Belt Jones *and also I was able to show the cinema going public my type of martial arts action in a film. And the film made near $20,000,000 for Warner Brothers.* Golden Needles *with Joe Don Baker and Burgess Meredith was a successful film too and then I did* Hot Potato *with me as the star again. Oscar Williams wrote that script and we filmed it in Thailand; that made a shed load of money too.*

So I knew I was making a lot of money for these people and I was not doing anymore films for just percentages, so after that, I started doing films for other people and worked with Fred Williamson and Jim Brown in Three the Hard Way, Take A Hard Ride *and* One Down Two to Go

And that's what it was like for me in the movie industry. The one thing I regret is that while I was in Hong Kong, Bruce and I talked about doing another film together and he wanted me to go back to Hong Kong to do another picture with him. That would have been one hell of an experience and I am sad that did not happen.

Williams (Jim Kelly) exercises in the moonlight while Lee goes on his first night time prowl.

BOB WALL
THE MAN WHO WAS OHARRA

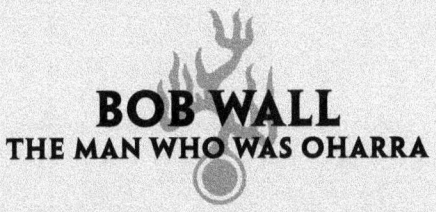

Robert Alan Wall was born in San Jose, California on 22nd August 1939, the second of six children. He married his wife Lillian on 16th November 1968 and they have two daughters, Shana Wall and Kara Desmond Wall, both of whom are actresses.

Wall began wrestling at San Jose State College in California, later moving to Los Angeles, where he trained in Judo-Jujitsu under Al Thomas. When Al Thomas moved to El Monte, Bob Wall began studying Okinawa-te Karate under Gordon Doversola. In 1965, still in Los Angeles, Bob Wall met Joe Lewis, a black belt in the Okinawan Shorin-Ryu style of Karate. When Bob Wall began working out with Joe Lewis, he realised that there had been something missing in his training; although he had worked hard, his skills were not where he thought they should have been. Bob Wall though it amazing what he had learned - just the interchange of ideas and thoughts with Joe Lewis - and added that he started understanding that knowledge was nothing more than the process of learning to think for yourself. This brought about his realisation that his training was supposed to be improving him as a human being; not just enabling him to go out and kick someone's butt.

In 1966, Bob Wall and Joe Lewis opened the Sherman Oaks Karate Studios in California. Soon after, Joe Lewis decided that he wanted to stop teaching and start, "doing other things."

With Lewis out, Bob Wall approached Chuck Norris, who agreed to go into a business partnership with him so in 1968, Joe Lewis sold his share of the business to Chuck Norris. then Bob Wall and Chuck Norris - who Wall would later called his 'main instructor' - began developing what became a highly successful chain of Karate studios across the US.

Bob Wall commented that Joe Lewis was very much into

training himself and if you got something out of the session, that was fine and if you didn't, that was your problem, whereas Chuck Norris, "really cared about bringing you along."

From 1965 to 1971, Bob Wall consistently placed second and third in every major US Karate tournament. In 1968, he won the middleweight titles of the US Championships in Dallas and the All-American Internationals in New York. Also in 1968, he won the Black Belt Championship (no weight division) at the Tournament of Champions in Fort Worth.

In 1970, Southern California promoter Lee Faulkner conceived the World Professional Team Championship and gathered together for the first time, Sport Karate's greatest fighters of the period, to form one team, which consisted of Joe Lewis, Chuck Norris, Mike Stone and Skipper Mullins, who voted unanimously to accept Bob Wall as the fifth member of the team. The quintet won the World Professional Team Championship title convincingly, defeating all those competitors that they came up against. The historic team even was held at the Long Beach Arena in California.

In 1972, when Bob Wall knew that Chuck Norris had a role in *The Way of the Dragon* and that Norris would be travelling to Rome and Hong Kong for the filming, he insisted on going along with him, being that the two of them were business partners. Bob Wall's insistence paid off for him as Bruce Lee said, "You're here, okay, I will put you in the movie." Initially though, Bruce Lee wasn't too pleased when the uninvited Bob Wall arrived in Rome. Bruce Lee reportedly asked, "Why did Norris bring this guy?".

On the day Bob Wall, Bruce Lee and Chuck Norris arrived in Hong Kong from Rome to film scenes for *The Way of the Dragon*, they appeared as guests on the HK TVB *Enjoy Yourself Tonight* show. Bob Wall and Chuck Norris did a Karate demonstration that started with Chuck Norris kicking a cigarette out of Bob Wall's mouth and then they sparred each other, highlighting skill in technique. The following day, via a local newspaper, someone challenged Chuck Norris.

In response to the challenge, Bob Wall went on the show the next night and addressed the audience. He said, "My instructor Chuck Norris is a much better fighter than I am, so I want you, whoever you are, to fight me first to see if you qualify to face him. Our fight will be held on this show so everyone in

Hong Kong can see it, because I'm going to beat you to death right here." Unsurprisingly, the challenger never responded and Chuck Norris has said that after that matter, he was never challenged in Hong Kong again.

Bob Wall described his fight scene with Bruce Lee in *The Way of the Dragon*, filmed in the New Territories just outside Hong Kong, as being where his character - a menacing, unholy, evil killer - is systematically taken apart by Bruce Lee's Tang Lung character. The same description could aptly be given to the Bob Wall/Bruce Lee tournament fight in *Enter the Dragon*, where Bob Wall's character, Oharra, Han's personal bodyguard, gets killed by Lee.

The scar-faced Oharra had been instrumental in the death of Lee's sister, Su Lin (Angela Mao Ying), and a big part of Lee's motive for going to the Island of Han, was to avenge his sister's death.

When Bruce Lee kicked Bob Wall with a side kick to the chest, sending him flying backwards into several of Han's men during the epic battle, such was the power of the kick, one of the stuntmen who caught him sustained a broken arm from the impact. *Enter the Dragon* Director, Robert Clouse, stated, "Bruce's fight scene with Bob Wall was all too real." Part of the scene involved Bob Wall smashing two bottles together and then advancing towards Bruce Lee with a broken bottle in each hand. There were no breakaway glass bottles in Hong Kong so real glass was used. Bruce Lee's reaction to Oharra's attack was to kick one of the bottles out of Bob Wall's hand and then follow up with further attacks. Bob Wall, reportedly, kept hold of the bottle instead of dropping it as rehearsed and Bruce Lee's hand hit the jagged edge of the broken bottle, causing a deep cut that needed twelve stitches.

According to Robert Clouse, the stuntmen began to say Bob Wall deliberately tried to hurt Bruce so they met with him that night and Bruce got caught up in their accusations. Robert Clouse added that Lee "had expressed outright antagonism toward the actor," and that his meeting with his stuntmen, he'd "agreed to exact revenge for this treacherous act." Robert Clouse stated he told Bruce Lee on the set that he had heard, "he meant to do Bob in," but they needed him to stay healthy for the good of the film as they needed him for more scenes to be shot in the US, when in actual fact, everything in the States

had already been shot. Robert Clouse explained Bruce Lee reluctantly agreed and told the stuntmen that, "Bob had to live for the good of the film."

Bob Wall responded, "The whole thing about Bruce trying to kill me was total crap fabricated by Bob Clouse for his book, so he could make money from it. Bruce and I were close friends and we both knew the dangers of using the real bottles. Clouse just wanted to make a buck at our expense."

Bob Wall stated that he trained several times with Bruce; at the Karate studio, at Bruce Lee's houses and on the sets of *The Way of the Dragon* and *Enter the Dragon*. 8mm home movie footage taken on the set of *Enter the Dragon* by co-star Ahna

Capri captures Bruce Lee 'attacking' Bob Wall with a succession of side-kicks during one of their practice or training sessions.

In 1974, referring to what he had witnessed the previous year during the making of *Enter the Dragon*, Bob Wall stated, "Normally, Bruce shunned challenges but one time in Hong Kong, a kid challenged him. He was sitting on a wall and he cursed Bruce in Chinese. He told Bruce that he was a phony, that he was just a movie Karate man and that he wasn't really a good martial artist. We were in between takes, so Bruce said 'Come on down and beat me up!' The kid jumped down and really started trying to take Bruce out. This kid was good. He

was no punk. He was strong and fast, and he was really trying to punch Bruce's brains in. But Bruce just methodically took him apart. He slammed the kid into a rock wall, then trapped him with his right knee and left hand. He took the kid's hand, punched in, just touched his cheek, brought his hand back, and said, 'See, you're mine'. He had the kid locked up! He couldn't move. He bloodied his mouth, got him up and rammed him into that wall about three more times just to show him that he could have him against that wall anytime he wanted. He made the kid fight until he couldn't move a muscle, and then he talked to him and said, 'This is a lesson for you. I want you to understand.' Bruce was doing it like a lesson! He told him, 'Look, your stance is too wide; you were doing this.' And then the kid shook his hand and said, 'You really are a master of the martial arts,' and he climbed back up on the wall."

In 1974, the same team that made *Enter the Dragon* (Producers Fred Weintraub and Paul Heller, and Director Robert Clouse) made *Black Belt Jones* with *Enter the Dragon* co-star Jim Kelly in the starring role. Bob Wall worked as the fight/stunt co-ordinator on the Warner Brothers film, as well as acting in it. He also assembled the group of black belts who appeared in the film including Pat Johnson, Sam Allred and Darnell Garcia.

By the mid-seventies, having "done everything there was to do in Karate", Bob Wall had walked away from the business of running Karate schools and focused more on real estate. A realtor from 1970, he was working one tenth as hard in that business, and making three times the money with the tax benefits and, as he explained, "I didn't have to be anything to anyone but me." In 1979, he formed Wall Street Properties.

Bob Wall continued to teach private lessons after giving up his schools, and remained involved in the martial arts in various sways. With his vast amount of work as a referee, announcer and guest commentator at US Karate tournaments in the 1970s, he became known as Bob 'The Voice of Karate' Wall.

In 1975, he authored the book *Who's Who in the Martial Arts and Directory of Black Belts*, the first reference work of its kind. Bob Wall established strict guidelines for entrance into the Who's Who. After testing the positive accomplishments of more than four hundred martial artists across the United States, 135 members were selected, eleven of whom were women.

In 1978, Game of Death - the film that Bruce Lee was

working on at the time of his death in 1973 - was completed using Bruce Lee lookalikes. It bore very little resemblance to Bruce Lee's original story and concept but made more money for Golden Harvest than all of Bruce Lee's previous films put together. Bob Wall had a supporting role in the film, again playing villain, Carl Miller, World Karate Champion and hitman for a syndicate headed by Dr. Land (Dean Jagger), that specialises in manipulating top talents in the entertainment industry. Bob Wall is the only American to have featured in three of Bruce Lee's films.

Bob Wall has had small roles in several films, including five films starring Chuck Norris (between 1985-92) and roles in fourteen episodes of Chuck Norris' *Walker, Texas Ranger* television series (between 1994-2001). In the 2009 film *Blood and Bone* starring Michael Jai White, Bob Wall played a personal bodyguard named O'Hara (sound familiar?).

Bob Wall's rivalry with Steven Seagal between 1988 and 1992 made headline news in the martial arts media. Bob Wall became offended and angered by Steven Seagal's disparaging remarks about Chuck Norris and other American martial artists and by Steven Seagal's boasts that he would fight to the death anybody who believed they could defeat him. Bob Wall gathered together a group of highly skilled, experienced martial artists, nicknamed the 'Dirty Dozen', to take up the challenge. This created controversy within the martial arts community, with many martial artists calling their response to Steven Seagal's comments an "over-reaction" and a "promotion of violence".

One of the 'Dirty Dozen', William 'Blinky' Rodriguez, declared that, "just by not accepting the challenge, Seagal tells us where he's at." The outcome? When Bob Wall and Steven Seagal met, Seagal apologised for making the offending comments and that was the end of the matter.

Bob Wall holds several black belts in separate disciplines of martial arts, including ninth degree black belts in American Tang Soo Do and Chun Kuk Do under Chuck Norris. Other notable masters Bob Wall has studied under include Gene LeBell (Judo) and the Machado Brothers (Brazilian Jiu-Jitsu). He is a co-founder and CEO of World Black Belt Inc., which was founded to unite a worldwide community of all ages, races and genders, by providing the best information, services and products in the world.

BOLO YEUNG
THE CHINESE HERCULES

Yang Sze, who would later change his name to Bolo Yeung, was born in 1946 to a local businessman and his wife in Guangzhou Suburbia, a suburb of Canton in Mainland China. Bolo began his martial arts training at the age of 10, where he studied under several Kung Fu masters and also trained in Wing Chun. In the 1960s, like millions of others, Yeung escaped the famine and communism of Mainland China by swimming 4km through the dirty Dapeng and Shenzhen Bays to Hong Kong. Growing up, he took an interest in bodybuilding and became a Bodybuilding Teacher in the 1960s. In 1967, he won the title Mr. Hong Kong Bodybuilding Champion and held it for ten years. He is also a former Mainland China powerlifting champion. Because of his impressively muscular physique and his huge pectoral muscles, he was chosen for several bad guy roles in films produced by Shaw Brothers Studios, such as *The Heroic Ones*, *The Deadly Duo*, *Angry Guest* and others, before leaving Sir Run Run Shaw's company in 1971. He stated, "In the 1970s, I was an action movie director in Hong Kong. During that time, the independent film was popular in Hong Kong. I left in 1971 and started to shoot my own films "

Bolo met Bruce Lee while the two were filming a Winston cigarette commercial. A friendship emerged and Bruce invited him to star in *Enter the Dragon*, where he became known as Bolo', the name of the character he portrayed. The two became close friends during the filming of *Enter the Dragon*, where Bruce and Bolo worked very closely on technique training and became a martial arts student of Bruce Lee for a short time. Bolo once stated in an interview, many years after Lee's death, "There will never be another Bruce Lee; and I am privileged to have had the honour of calling him a friend." He was wrongly described in the films blurb for *Enter the Dragon* as being the South East Asian Shotokan Karate Champion, he never even practiced that martial art and for years and right up to today they still believe he is a champion in this art. Some people still believe he had a fight in the movie with Bruce Lee. Again, this is untrue; it was just a set of publicity photos taken to promote the film, though there was a rumour that Lee had said to Bolo that he would fight and kill him in his next movie *The Game of Death*, but this was never to be proved as Lee died before he got to finish this movie. He still retains the barbell Bruce Lee kept in his Golden Harvest office along with a rare business card from Lee's Hong Kong production company Concord Productions that he treasures as a memento of his friendship with Lee. He said, "During the filming of *Enter the Dragon*, Bruce and I worked very closely on technique training. We experimented, trying to decide what worked and what wouldn't. You see, Bruce was always learning, always experimenting, and always changing".

When asked what kind of person Bruce Lee was, Bolo said, "A lot people ask me about Bruce, especially foreigners. What kind of person he was? He was a man with special thoughts. He was affable to people working for him. He drove a Mercedes-Benz but crouched in the dust playing poker with his staff. But when meeting his boss, he was always the one sitting while his boss standing. The characters he portrayed in his movies were all heroes. They were powerful, but simple. In real life, Bruce Lee was a person with deep inside. He thought about a lot of things nothing to do with martial art. Such as where are we from and what we come to this world for? Is there a God or any higher power? Is there metempsychosis? What he advocated was 'add to it'. Add a bit to your energy, skill and spirit and so on. Everything needs to be added on a bit every day. Thus people can progress. He was always looking for the next breakthrough. Those who can deny themselves and often make breakthroughs will never be defeated and never be eliminated. Most of people are even not brave enough to question the tradition. How could they be supposed to question the rules they are executing for decades? Why do we bother thinking about these things? What will we get to research them? Is there any commercial benefit? No! As a martial art master, it is more realistic to open more martial are academies to earn more money. So, why do we explore these things? The martial art needs people to push to progress. We have to break the boundary of the rigid criterion, outdated traditions and all which prevent martial art from progressing. Bruce Lee thought in different way. His way is advancing when the enemy advances."

During the 1970s and '80s, Bolo starred in numerous Kung Fu films and dabbled in directing. His first film was *Fists of Justice* (1977) and his second was *Writing Kung Fu* (1979). Remembering these times Bolo said, "At that time, action movies were mainly martial arts; kicking and boxing only, without heavy weapons. Even blades and swords were rarely appeared in the movies until Tsui Hark made his *Warriors from the Magic Mountain* in 1983.Then there were action comedies; Jackie Chan started to show up on the screen with *Drunken Master* (1978) and *Snake in Eagle's Shadow* (1976)"

Throughout the eighties, he would appear in a number of Hong Kong action films, particularly those starring Sammo Hung. Notable examples include *My Lucky Stars* (1985), *Millionaire's Express* (1986) and *Where's Officer Tuba?* (1986), but his breakout film was *Bloodsport*, based on the allegedly true story of Frank Dux. Shot on a US $1.5million budget, it became a US box-office hit in the spring of 1988. Jean-Claude Van Damme had the leading role as Frank Dux, while Bolo Yeung played the role of Chong Li. A strong friendship formed between the two actors on the set of *Bloodsport*; and Van Damme

Bruce Lee discussing his vision for Yang Sze's fight scene.

wanted no one but Bolo to play opposite him in his film *Double Impact*, which was set in the Orient. Thinking back to those times recently Bolo said, "I went to the Hollywood in 1986 for the movie *Bloodsport*. It was the first movie that Jean-Claude Van Damme and I worked together. I acted a very bad guy in that movie. It was Jean-Claude Van Damme's first movie to act the leading role and he really had his name up with that movie. After that, it was *Double Impact* in 1990, with Jean-Claude Van Damme again".

Canadian action film actor, director and producer Jalal Merhi met Bolo in Hong Kong while shooting his first film *Fearless Tiger*, then again on the set of *Double Impact*. Jalal was impressed with his personality and ability, and decided to create a part specifically for Bolo. Later Merhi worked with Yeung on more films such as *Tiger Claws*, *TC 2000* and *Tiger Claws 2*. *The Fists, the Kicks and the Evil* (1979) was his favourite film from that era.

In 1986, Bolo made a cameo appearance in the

Bruce Lee demonstrates how he wants Yang Sze to deal with the incompetent guards as stuntman Mars stands with his back to camera.

Yang Sze and Bruce Lee in a publicity shot for *Enter the Dragon*.

Hong Kong action film *Legacy of Rage* starring Brandon Lee (Bruce Lee's son) alongside Michael Wong and Regina Kent, in his first martial arts action movie, directed by Ronny Yu. He was one of the very few people to star with both of the Lees in a movie.

He was always stereotyped as a villain until he got the chance to play the good guy in *Shootfighter: Fight to the Death* (1993). He played the good guy in three more movies: *Shootfighter II* (1996), *TC 2000* (1993), and *Ironheart* (1992) and *Fearless Tiger* (1991).

In 2007, Bolo made a rare appearance as a protagonist in *Blizhniy Boy: The Ultimate Fighter*. Jalal Merhi directed the first 60 minutes of the film that was shot in Toronto, but due to other commitments could not complete the remaining part of the film in Russia. Producer Erken Ialgashev directed the remainder of the film. Due to legal issues, the film remains unreleased.

Now he currently lives in Monterey Park, a city in Los Angeles, California, where he still regularly trains at his local gym, but his preferred martial art these days is Tai Chi, although he still studies and practices other martial arts and bodybuilding, which is still an integral part of his life and career. He has two sons, Danny and David Yeung, and a daughter, Debora. He still likes to go to the gym, especially LA Fitness and trains alongside his son David, who is a bodybuilding champion in his own right.

He is the Chairman of the Hong Kong Gym Business Association, and the Team Manager of the Taipei International Bodybuilders Squad.

When asked about martial arts, he responded, "How do we judge whether a thing is right or wrong? We should look at its purpose. What the purpose of martial art? Is it for a healthy body? Is it for good moral? Is it for better self-restraint? Each of them is the purpose of martial art but none of them is the ultimate one. The ultimate purpose of the martial art is to defeat your enemy at quickly as possible. If this is the ultimate purpose of martial art, we have the reason to think about whether the way of modern athletic wushu taolu (the name for a modern sport similar to gymnastics involving the performance of adapted Chinese bare-handed and weapons forms judged to a set of contemporary aesthetic criteria for points) is correct or not."

He recently stated his feelings towards Tai Chi and Qui

Gong "Why do we always defend? Tai Chi never actively attacks. The art of war says "Retreating when the enemy advances". Qui Gong is difficult and complicated. Basically, it is concerning breath. People don't know the correct way to breathe. When I have no movie to make I still practice martial art a lot. It is not working if you just start practising 3 months before the shooting. It is impossible to show people your best in 3 months.

Finally on his success Bolo said "I think that all started with Bruce Lee and Enter the Dragon. All the fans and audiences from 20 years ago still remember Bruce lee as the biggest star. They still have not found anyone to take his place. Also, it helped to work with Jean Claude Van Damme on his movies. Like Bruce lee, Jean-Claude offered a special package, a unique look that attracted and kept audiences coming back. It's work, whether I'm the hero or the villain. I'm not a kid anymore, where nervousness keeps me from sleeping. I have always been happy being the bad guy.

Bruce Lee was the King of Kung Fu and Angela Mao, the Martial Arts Queen, but neither could compare or compete with the Ultimate Chinese Hercules that is Bolo Yeung.

Yang Sze and Bruce Lee in a publicity shot for Enter the Dragon.

ANGELA MAO YING
THE FIRST LADY OF KUNG FU

Angela Mao Ying was born in Taiwan in 20th September 1950. She is the daughter of Mao Yung Kang, a Peking Opera star, who escaped China to Taiwan in 1949.

At the age of 5, Angela Mao was enrolled into an Opera School in Taiwan. One of her classmates was James Tien (*The Big Boss*, *Fist of Fury*) who also went on to become an actor for Golden Harvest films. She went on and trained at the school for the next 14 years. Angela also attended ballet classes before joining The Fu Shing Peking Opera in 1958.

Mao trained in Hapkido at an early age, as well as other martial arts, both of which would later help her achieve success in martial arts movies. In 1969, at the age of 17, Golden Harvest director Huang Feng (who also discovered Sammo Hung and Carter Wong) was looking for a young woman who knew martial arts to be the leading lady for his upcoming sword fighting film, *Angry River*. This was to be Golden Harvest's first production.

With her experience in acting and martial arts, Angela quickly began taking leading roles in other action movies for Golden Harvest, including *Hapkido*, *Lady Whirlwind*, and *The Fate of Lee Khan* (directed by the late King Hu). She was also successful in other movies such as *The Association*, *The Himalayan*, and a number of others. Despite their success, her films were not being released in America, and because of this, she was unknown to the western movie audience.

This would soon change in 1973.

Internationally, she found fame for her role as the doomed sister of Bruce Lee's character in 1973's *Enter the Dragon*. She was only paid $100 dollars for her short role in this movie. Although Bruce Lee died shortly after the production of the movie, Mao was able to train and develop a friendship with Lee, although she was not able to attend his funeral as she was in

Taipei at the time.

Following the incredible success of her small but memorable role in *Enter the Dragon,* many of her previous films began to be released in the west. *Hapkido* was the first to gain this wider audience. The film also starred Carter Wong, Sammo Hung, and her real life teacher Whang In Sik, as well as Chi Hon Tsoi. Also working on *Hapkido* was an unaccredited 'boot master,' Leung Siu-Leung - now better known as Jackie Chan - who assisted Sammo with the fight choreography and who would later work as a stuntman on *Enter the Dragon*.

Mao continued with a string of successful movies through the seventies. Angela, along with actor Carter Wong, became a bit of a Kung Fu duo in a series of classic martial arts movies. One of their best movies was *When Taekwondo Strikes*, which apart from having possibly the best title of any Kung Fu film, was also the only film ever made by the father of American Taekwondo, Jhoon Rhee. Mao spent time training with Rhee during the making of this movie.

She left Golden Harvest in the late 70's and made a few more Taiwanese productions including *Two Great Cavaliers*, *Scorching Sun* and *Duel of Death*.

She retired in 1980 at the young age of 30 and married her long time boyfriend, Kelly

Angela Mao and Bruce Lee in discussion towards the end of her scene in *Enter the Dragon*.

Angela Mao gives Bruce Lee her opinion during a break in filming on *Enter the Dragon*.

Robert Clouse, Angela Mao and Bruce Lee in discussions about her fight scene.

Lau and devoted herself to her family.

Mao has been presented with a Honorary Second Degree Black Belt in Hapkido in recognition of her work in promoting the art of Hapkido to the world, and for being the art's most honourable, heroic, and beautiful female representative.

Bruce Lee gives Robert Clouse his ideas on Angela Mao's final scene in Enter the Dragon.

Bruce Lee and Robert Clouse discuss the chase scene between Oharra's gang and Angela Mao in *Enter the Dragon*.

SAMMO HUNG
THE DYNAMIC MAESTRO

Sammo Hung was born on in Hong Kong on 7th January 1952. He started at a young age at the main opera academy Yu Jim Yuen in 1959, after his grandparents had agreed for him to go to study there. His school friends were Jackie Chan and Yuen Biao who were also preparing to become actors in the Peking Opera. Hung had to leave the academy after a serious injury that left him bedridden for a long time, during which time he put on a considerably amount of weight.

Hung's acting career began while he was training in acrobatics, martial arts and dance as a child at the China Drama Academy. He made his feature film debut as an actor at the age of 12, but it was not until 1970 when his career began in earnest as he started working for Raymond Chow's Golden Harvest film company. At first, he was hired as a choreographer for *The Fast Sword* (1970). Hung's popularity soon began to increase, and because of the quality of his choreography and disciplined approach to his work, he was chosen by King Hu to choreograph two of his greatest films; *A Touch of Zen* (1971) and *The Fate of Lee Khan* (1973).

Hung's big break as a film actor came with a role as a sparring partner in the Bruce Lee film *Enter the Dragon* (1973) as he fights Bruce in the opening sequence. He recalled that this was the last fight scene that Lee shot before his untimely death on 20th July 1973.

Hung established his reputation as a skilled physical comedian in several Kung Fu comedies, beginning with 1978s *Enter the Fat Dragon*.

After the success of Jackie Chan in *Drunken Master* (1978), Hung was hired to make a similar film with prominent star Simon Yuen. As Chan's fame grew, it was expected that Sammo could surpass him in popularity and succeed with the film called *Magnificent Butcher* (1979), in which he played Lam Sai-Wing,

a disciple of Wong Fei Hung. During filming, Yuen Hsiao Tien died of a heart attack and was replaced by Fan Mei Sheng. It was thought that his absence from the film was likely to lead to low sales of the title, but today it is recognised as one of the best Kung Fu movies of all time.

As Hung's star began to rise, he used his influence to assist his former opera classmates, with regular collaborations with Jackie Chan and Yuen Biao as well as others such as Yuen Wah who also began to make appearances in his films.

In 1978 and 1981, Hung made two films which are regarded as two of the best examples of movies incorporating Wing Chun. The first was *Warriors Two* with the Korean actor Casanova Wong, who has the final fight with Sammo.

Hung's choreography, set in urban areas, was more realistic and frantic. The fight sequences of several of these films, such as Winners *and Sinners* (1982) and *Wheels on Meals*

Sammo Hung and Bruce Lee face off in the opening scene of *Enter the Dragon*.

(1985) came to define the style of the 80s martial arts movies

Hung also created the genre of *Encounters of the Spooky Kind* (1981) and *The Dead and the Deadly* (1983). Both films show vampires who, as rigid bodies, moving jumping, and Taoist priests who are able to repress these vampires

In the mid-1980s, Sammo started Bo Ho films, a film company that operated under the Golden Harvest banner. Films made by Bo Ho include *Mr. Vampire* (1985), and *On the Run* (1989) and *Heart of Dragon* (1985).

He directed *Once Upon a Time in China and America* (1997), his first film shot in the US. Hung is not particularly well-known in the west as an actor, but in the late 90s, Sammo Hung took to stardom an American television series *Martial Law* (1998-2000). With Arsenio Hall as his co-star, Sammo has become one of Hong Kong's greatest, yet unusual, success stories.

AHNA CAPRI
THE MADAM OF HAN'S ISLAND

Ahna Capri was born Anna Marie Nanasi July 6, 1944 in Budapest, Hungary. She made her film debut in the western *Outlaw's Son*. Ahna achieved her greatest enduring popularity as the enticing Tania in the exciting martial arts cult classic *Enter the Dragon*. Capri also gave an excellent and impressive performance as country singer Rip Torn's snobby, fed-up girlfriend Mayleen in the terrific film *Payday*.

Ahna's other memorable movie roles include the terrified Nicky in the creepy Devil worship horror winner *The Brotherhood of Satan*; feisty wildlife photographer Terry in *Piranha*; and luscious assassin Londa Wyeth in the tacky Crown International exploitation romp *The Specialist*. Among the many TV shows Capri guested in were Ms. Columbo, *Baretta, Kojak, Police Story, Cannon, Mannix, Ironside, Adam-12, The Mod Squad, The Invaders, The Wild, Wild West, I Spy, The Man from

Ahna Capri and Bruce Lee share a joke in between filming.

Tania (Ahna Capri) entertains the guests of the banquet on the first day on Han's island.

Ahna Capri poses for a photograph on the tournament chairs.

U.N.C.L.E., Branded, Leave it to Beaver, and Maverick.

During the filming of Enter the Dragon, Capri became close friends with co-stars Bob Wall, Bruce Lee, John Saxon and Jim Kelly. Wall, closest to Ahna in the days before her passing, explained that anyone who came into contact with her knew he was in the presence of someone very special.

Ahna Capri sadly passed away on 19th 2010 from injuries she sustained in a car accident. "She brought a light to our experience while filming Enter the Dragon and she will be missed greatly," as her former co-star Bob Wall.

Before her death, Capri was able to share with the world, something she had kept to herself for over thirty years; 8mm footage she filmed on the set of Enter the Dragon...

Tania (Anna Capri) - The madame of Han's island.

THE 8MM FILM FOOTAGE

During the filming of *Enter the Dragon* Ahna Capri shot some film footage on a newly acquired 8mm camera for her own personal collection. The exact amount of footage had been established as 15 minutes and some time ago, an enthusiastic fan put the footage he had on YouTube for all to see and although it was slightly out of focus, it was watchable and gave the viewer an idea of the content of this footage. It was then immediately removed by "Matsuda Seiko" from Japan. Whether he is actually the person who acquired the rights to the 8mm footage that belonged to Ahna Capri, it doesn't really matter at this time. However, we do know that the footage now is in the hands of a private Japanese collector who paid a large sum of money to own the footage.

One thing we know is that three minutes of the footage was used in the documentary *Blood and Steel* which featured in the Warner Brothers Two-Disc Special Edition DVD and 40th Anniversary Blu-ray version of *Enter the Dragon*.

Over the years, we have seen many photos taken of Bruce Lee on the set of *Enter the Dragon* but these shots did not appear in the final film as they were most likely practice sessions where Bruce was seeing what would or would not work on film. With the help of Ahna Capri's 8mm footage, we see some of these training sessions, which gives a great window as to how the film was made. Not all the shots are of Bruce Lee; there are some of John Saxon, Jim Kelly and others that were in the film.

Most of the footage is from the tennis courts which were used as the tournament grounds on Han's Island. Also, there is footage of the Hotel Bella Vista Ahna must have visited whilst filming *Enter the Dragon*.

With this taster, we look at who Ahna Capri was, the history of the Hotel Bella Vista, how the footage came into existence, what it consisted of, and how some of it ended up in *Blood and Steel*.

How did the footage come into existence?

Back in Ahna's early career days, she loved going on location and she had told her agent at that particular time that she wanted to go anywhere on location because her mother had just passed away and she would welcome the opportunity to work out of town. So her agent called her up and said, "You wanted to go on location; is Hong Kong far enough," so she asked, "What are you talking about?" "There is a film called *Enter the Dragon* and its starring a martial artist called Bruce Lee," said her agent, "Have you ever head of him?" "No," she replied, "I have never heard of Bruce Lee or martial arts." He agent then asked her, "Would you like to go to Hong Kong?" to which she replied, "Absolutely. When should I go?" "Tonight," said her agent. "No way," was Ahna's response. When she asked him what her part in the movie was going to be, his reply was, "No frigging idea but they will send you the script. Just pack your luggage and get on that plane." She somehow miraculously made it onto a China Airlines midnight flight going to Hong Kong.

Ahna's father had given her a compact super 8mm film camera for her birthday a couple of months before she left for Hong Kong and she threw it in her bag just before she left, thinking she could use it for something to do and to pass the time whilst on set. She use the camera several times during the film shoot, just walking around taking some shots of Bruce Lee, John Saxon, Jim Kelly and Bob Wall. In hindsight, she was sorry that she did not take more but when finished and processed, she had the five three-minute sections spliced together so that it would be easier to view and show her friends. It was all done just for fun and it did not have a beggining, a middle or an end. She later remembered that she mainly filmed when it was the tournament scenes and when she first arrived on the film set. It was just up some steps to where they filmed the tournament scenes and she also remembered an interesting fact that she was invited to a formal lunch at a rich palatial estate on a Sunday afternoon. After arriving, lunch was held on a boat which was at the bottom of the steps from this palace and she noticed some big yellow flags flapping in the wind so she asked her host what were all the yellow flags were doing there. He said, "Tomorrow, some movie company is going to start shooting here for the next two to three weeks and it's a film starring Bruce Lee," two which she replied, "I cannot believe that I am the leading lady of that movie!"

THE HOTEL BELLA VISTA

In Ahna's footage we see scenes from the Hotel Bella Vista which she visited. Sitting atop Penha Hill, the stately Hotel Bella Vista is one of the most recognised landmarks in the Portuguese colony of Macau; not just for its architectural beauty, but for its colourful 120-year-old history. In that time, the building has transformed many times over; from private home, school, refugee centre, and modest hotel. In its current lavish and stunning incarnation, the landmark is intentionally intimate and private. The building was constructed on the hilltop facing the Praya Grande as was tradition in Macau for public buildings or those of wealthy merchants. The Consul Residence, the former Bella Vista - translated as 'Beautiful View' - was part of the Mandarin Hotel Group chain and was built in 1870s for a Macanese family.

In 1890, a British Naval Officer bought the building as a retreat inn for Hong Kong Expatriates that came to Macau as a place for rest. From 1917 to 1923, it was used as Liceu - a Macanese High School - and was one of several buildings used as a refugee centre during the Second World War. Three years after the war ended, it opened as a hotel where it operated until 1999, when it became the residence of the Portuguese Consul in Macau.

AHNA CAPRI'S 8MM FOOTAGE

Here is a numbered Shot by Shot breakdown of Ahna Capri's 8mm film footage, described to the best of what can be seen:

1. Bob Wall kicks a shield with his left leg three times on the tennis courts, whilst Jim Kelly holds the shield for him.
2. Bob Wall performs two jumping back spin kicks, again with his left leg. Jim Kelly stands in front of him as his sparring partner, but does not hold up a shield for him.
3. Jim Kelly does two side kicks toward Bob Wall, who is now holding a kicking shield.
4. Robert Clouse is in the foreground and Andre Morgan to the right hand side of the picture. Clouse walks across picture and pulls a funny face at Ahna's camera when he walks off. From

THE 50TH ANNIVERSARY COMPANION

ENTER THE DRAGON

left to right of the picture are Raymond Chow, Andre Morgan and Fred Weintraub having a conversation on the set.

5. Shih Kien is on the throne as the camera pans to reveal Jim Kelly and two stuntmen being directed by Robert Clouse.

6. Bruce Lee is on the left hand side of the screen with his hands in the on-guard position as a stuntman in a yellow Karate uniform stands in front of him. He kicks him twice and the stuntman bounces back up. Lee now steps back and moves backwards and forwards with his hands on his hips, talking about how the shot has worked.

7. We now see a long shot of the same take but this time Lee kicks the stuntman, who flips back up and kicks Lee. It is obvious to see that this is the choreography rehearsals for the Roper/Bolo fight.

8. Lee laughs to camera with his arms folded. He moves around, spitting into his hands as if spitting out teeth as he talks and laughs with the stuntmen, surrounded by Karate-suited extras.

9. Lee is demonstrating and practising one of the kicks that Roper has to perform against Tony Liu. He repeats this shot four times in various wide to close up shots.

10. John Saxon is to the right of the picture talking to Bob Wall, though only the back of his head is visible. Jim Kelly is also in the conversation, wearing dark sunglasses to the left of the picture.

11. Bruce Lee is to the right of the picture talking to John Saxon.

12. The camera shows a side shot of Hans's throne with Bruce Lee at the far end, as the guards practice the morning ritual.

13. There are nine shots of Ahna Capri on the right hand side of the screen, standing near Han's throne, Lee is on the throne talking to Ahna, laughing and joking with her between takes. Shih Kein is sat in Han's chair. This footage was most likely filmed by David Friedman, the Warner Brothers stills photographer.

14. This follow-on shot now has Lee standing and walking around as Robert Clouse is directing a scene.

15. The footage cuts to a shot showing a windy day. From left to right, we see Raymond Chow and Andre Morgan as Bruce assists Ahna as she puts her coat on.

16. In the final shot of this sequence, we see Bruce stretching his left leg and then walking with Ahna towards the throne.

17. The next ten shots show different distant-shot angles as they await the filming of the big battle scene to begin.

18. Ahna, looking very cold, is seen talking to Bob Clouse.

19. Back to the throne scene as Ahna is again talking to Robert Clouse.
20. John Saxon is on the left and Shih Kien is on the right as they eat the prop grapes between them.
21. Bruce is with Bolo Yeung, directing the fight scene with the incompetent guards; Bruce is also in conversation with a stuntman called Mars.
22. Another shot with Shih Kien and John Saxon from a different angle with Betty Chung (Mai Ling) in-between them.
23. The camera captures two excellent shots from a different angle to the main camera and nearly shows the whole scene where Bolo deals with the incompetent guards.
24. Jim Kelly is on the right of the screen with Peter Archer on the left in an on-guard position. The tennis court walls are in the background as Archer launches a front kick at Jim Kelly, who blocks and steps out of range.
25. In the same locale but moving round slightly, Kelly is on left, as he machine-gun kicks parsons three times, each time blocking Kelly's kick.
26. In this shot, there are three people. From the left of the screen is an unknown then executive assistant Madalena Chan plus Bob Wall with his scar. Bob then brings his hands up and makes a comical wave.
27. Again in the same locale as Kelly and Archer, we see Bruce on the right and Bob Wall on the left. Bruce now executes four of his powerful side kicks towards Wall, which he avoids by going back very quickly. It looks like a practice session for their fight together. Jim Kelly is in the background.
28. A close up of Bruce doing the same thing, followed by a shot where the camera has panned out again and Bruce asks everyone to move back.
29. Following this are two shots of Ahna standing in the scene were the prisoners attack the guards on the battle ground as she makes a haste retreat.
30. In this shot, Ahna walks across the set with extras. Smiling around, she goes and talks to John Saxon.
31. The shot is of the boat landing where Roper, Lee and Williams get off the junk. We first see the back of the head of make-up lady Kuo Hsiung Chen, followed by a group sitting down to have a chat on the jetty as the camera zooms down to them.
32. The next is a pan shot of the crew on the jetty. It then moves up from the sea shore up to the small roundhouse and then up to the tennis club house.
33. Lee is in the centre of the screen with Jim Kelly to his left.

John Saxon is in front of Bruce and bent forward whilst the make-up lady does his hair.

34. The camera is focused on the junk at sea before it pans down to the smaller boat. It then focuses on Jim Kelly on the jetty, who, on cue, walks up the jetty, followed by John Saxon, and then by Lee, as they all set off up towards Han's Island.

35. Two shots of Ahna playing dead.

36. The following three shots are of Ahna relaxing on the set. The final shot in this series is of Ahna hugging the make-up lady Kuo Hsiung Chen.

37. A downward panning shot from high up on the shore of the jetty. As the crew are working and setting up the jetty shot, the camera pans backwards and forwards to the boarding boat

38. Shot of the make-up lady Kuo Hsiung Chen on the balcony of what could be Hotel Bella Vista.

39. The shot shows the sea dock for the Macau Hydrofoil boat.

40. This shot is of the Hydrofoil boat leaving the dock and going to Macau.

41. Five shots of the Hotel Bella Vista, plus pan shots of the views from the hotel.

42 .This is a different camera angle for the opening sequence of the Lee/Oharra fight. Bruce is on the left and Bob wall on the right.

43. Again a different camera shot of Lee/Oharra, but in a similar position to the one that was used in the film. The shot contains most of the opening sequence.

44. John Saxon is on the left and Bruce on the right, who has a silver thermos drinks cup in his hand with a jacket round his shoulders.

45. Close up of Fred Weintraub smiling.

46. Pan shot from Hotel Bella Vista of the view from the hotel of the bay.

47. The shot is now of the Lee/Oharra fight but a bit further on, we see Bruce lying down on the floor and kicking Wall in the groin, followed by one shot of him kicking Wall down and one shot of the final side kick to the body that pushes Bob into the crowd, tipping him over the chairs.

48. John Saxon sat down in a chair and having a discussion with executive assistant Madalena Chan behind him.

49. A close up of Jim Kelly's mouth.

50. A close up of John Saxon's mouth and tongue as he tries to blow bubbles with some chewing gum.

51. Bolo Yeung warming up doing body twists.

52. Bruce performs some Cha Cha moves to the camera.

53. Bruce with John Saxon on the set just before the Bolo fight as both the cameras and boom microphone are in shot.

54. Robert Clouse walks across the set as Bruce is in the background directing the fight scene. Clouse fools around mocking Bruce's Cha Cha moves.

55. Pan shot of the bay from the tennis courts, where the tournament is being held.

56. Two fantastic shots of Bruce in full martial arts action against Han. This is a different camera position to the one used in the film and you see Bruce really going for it and only stopping when an extra misses his mark.

57. John Saxon with Han's bear claw on his shoulder.

58. Another fantastic shot of Bruce in full action against Han's Guards.

59 Pan shot across the tournament ground, ending with Ahna Capri sat in Han's throne chair.

60 The final shot is another pan shot of the tournament's tennis courts where most of Ahna Capri's *Enter the Dragon* 8mm footage was taken.

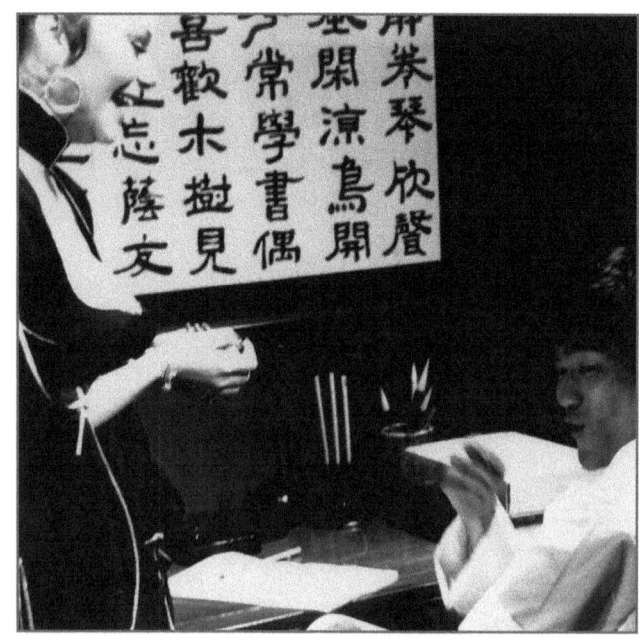

Ahna Capri and Bruce Lee share a joke at the desk of his room in *Enter the Dragon*.

So a full breakdown of all the footage that was on You Tube; around eighty shots of different lengths, each ranging from a couple of seconds to half a minute. When Ahna was in the shot during the footage, it was most likely that Dave Friedman, the Warner Brothers stills photographer, was filming her.

So you have some of this footage and some of it you may never see, but at least you will know most of its contents and will have an idea of what it contained. As an additional note, the footage was out of focus so some information might not be fully accurate.

HOW THE FOOTAGE WAS USED IN DOCUMENTARIES

The footage was first discovered by Walt Missingham, an Australian film producer many years back. Ahna had it with a bunch of other Super 8 footage, but it was not until she learned of its value from Walt, that she decided to develop the footage, entrusting it to Missingham to do so.

After agreement with Ahna, a promoter - having been introduced to Ahna through Bob Wall - showed the footage at several conventions and the fans went wild. Tsuyoshi Abe eventually bought the footage from Ahna, before selling it through a mediator to another party in Japan.

When the time came it came time to include a new documentary on a new Warner Brothers *Enter the Dragon* DVD, there was nothing new for the fans to see. Paul Heller wanted to make the story about Weintraub, himself and the behind the scenes, but this was rejected as the main interest had always been Bruce. So three minutes of the Ahna Capri footage was licensed for the project *Blood and Steel: The Making of Enter the Dragon* and it was a hit!

The Super 8 footage is now in Japan, but the Capri estate owns the rights in the US for conventions, stills for books, etc.

There is an extra six minutes of footage that is still in Ahna's archive, which she always wanted to hold onto, so therefore did not show it all. Her sister is believed to own her estate now, so if this footage is ever to get a proper release, it is her who people will have to deal with.

PETER ARCHER
PARSONS

Peter Ian Archer was born 8th July 1948 in Queensland to Alexander (Sandy) and June Archer. Having grown up on a farm, Archer had a down-to-earth personality - no matter the accomplishments he achieved throughout his short life. He would always joke that "you could take the boy out of the bush, but you can never take the bush out of the boy".

Peter soon found he had a passion for martial arts and went and studied Goju Ryu Karate in Seigo Tada's Odokan in Hong Kong, under Shogi Yuki. He eventually gained a black belt in both Goju-ryu and Shotokan Karate.

Around late 1972 to early 1973, Archer had become a very successful Karate champion in Hong Kong. During one of the many tournaments Bruce Lee attended. He approached Peter after watching him fight. "Would you like to be in my film?", asked Bruce. "Sure," Peter responded, "What as?"

"Not sure," Bruce replied, "I'll write something in for you."

And indeed he did write something in for him. That film was *Enter the Dragon* and Peter got the role as New Zealand's competitior, with the memorable lines:

Parsons: *Do I bother ya!*
Lee: *Don't waste yourself*
Parsons: *What's your style?*
Lee: *My style? You can call it the art of fighting without fighting.*
Parsons: *The art of fighting without fighting? Show me some of it.*
Lee: *Later*

As the scene evolves, Parsons gets onto a small boat which, due to the large waves, begins to sink. The insinuation in the film that Parsons could drown, was not written into the original script. The little boat was released, as per the script, but the film production team didn't realise the boat had a leak in it. As the boat started to sink, the film crew panicked. "Don't worry! Get the shot; I can swim!" cried Archer, being an Australian who grew up around water. The director kept filming and the boat continued to sink into the water. Archer reminisced, "It was fine as I was a strong swimmer, but gee, that sea stank! I was covered in it." Sadly, Archer's voice was dubbed by another actor. The director did not feel that Archer's voice was "New Zealand" enough, though the dubbed voice sounded nothing like a New Zealander's accent either.

Peter drew a bit of a short straw as his tournament fight, against Jim Kelly's Williams, he takes quite a beating as Williams emerges victorious. What are really interesting to see are behind-the-scenes photos showing Bruce painstakingly choreographing the match with Peter and Jim.

Archer remembered Lee to be a deeply philosophical man, who loved to discuss and break down the philosophies behind martial arts and life itself. Lee and Archer enjoyed their filmmaking experience together, with Lee reportedly asking Archer to be in his next film. However, neither knew that this film was to be Lee's last.

After fighting in Hong Kong and becoming a Karate champion, Peter moved away from martial arts and began a business career. In 1975, he started Jackel Australia, a company which marketed and distributed baby and dye products in Australia, becoming the sole Australian and New Zealand Tommee Tippee licensee. He was also the creator of the Zoggs Swimwear brand and was a passionate entrepreneur.

Sadly, Peter Archer died of cancer on 13th April 2000.

Jim Kelly and Peter Archer rehearse their fight scene.

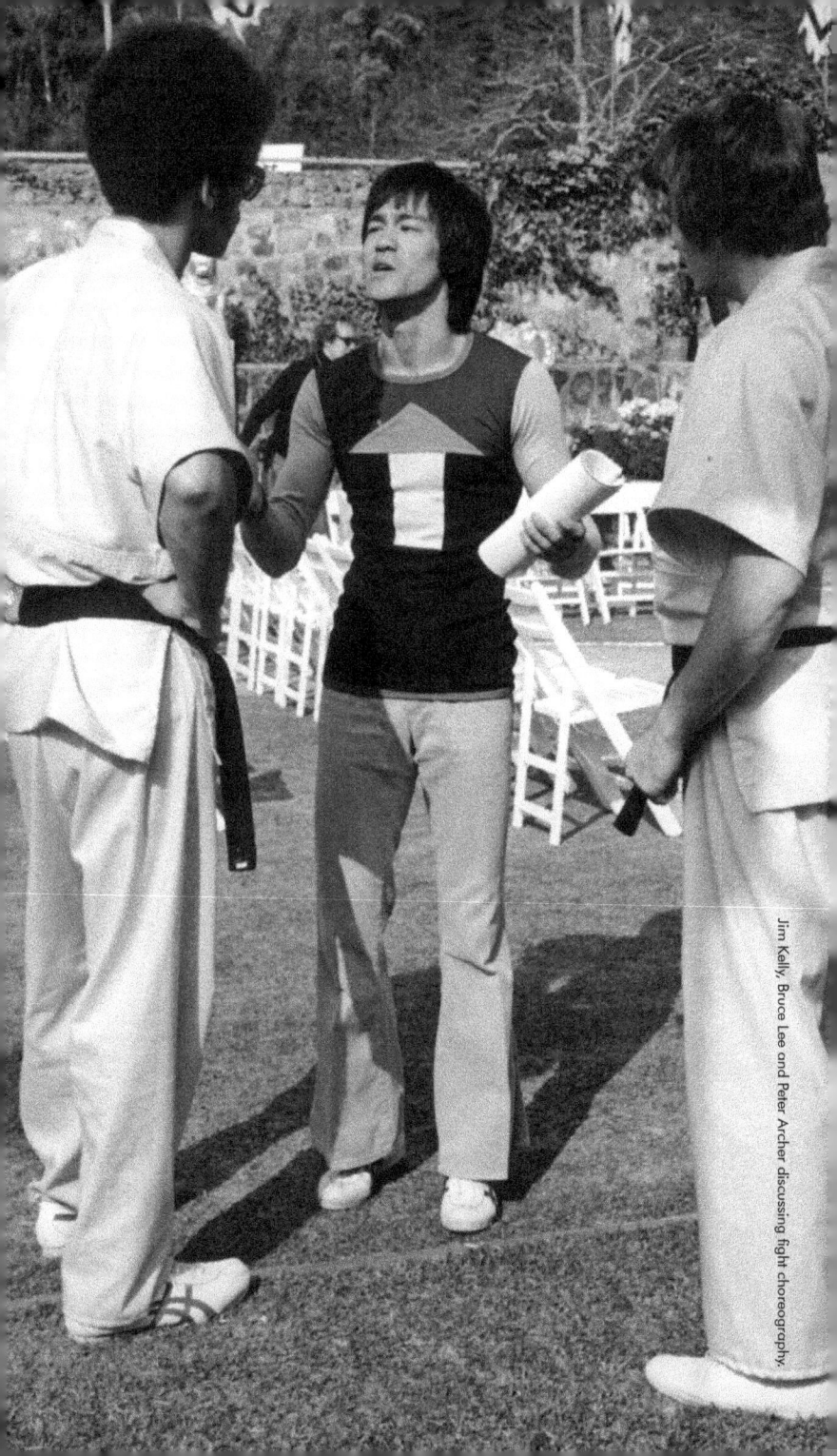
Jim Kelly, Bruce Lee and Peter Archer discussing fight choreography.

Bruce Lee shows Peter Archer how he wants him to throw a punch at Jim Kelly.

GEOFFREY WEEKS
BRAITHWAITE

Geoffrey Weeks was born in 1922 and during his younger days, he toured India as a member of the Entertainments National Service Association, learning his trade as an announcer and commentator. His training landed him a career in radio and in the late 1940s, he could be heard on the station, Radio Delhi. Later, he was based in Hong Kong as a radio host with Hong Kong Television and Radio's Radio 3 station. By 1972, he was the head of English radio on Hong Kong Radio. Weeks once had Nick Bailey from the famous British "Boat That Rocked" pirate station, Radio Caroline audition for him.

As was typical with all gweilo (Cantonese slang for westerners), when a film crew hit Hong Kong, they looked for locals to appear in films to give the film a balance against the Chinese community. Geoffrey was a well know figure in the Foreign Correspondence Club, and therefore was an easy casting choice for the producers of Enter The Dragon.

Weeks has only three small scenes in the movie, however each of the scenes have lines that are well remembered by appreciators of the film. Memorable lines include, "We would like you to attend a tournament of martial arts," "Any damn fool can pull a trigger," and "Put your Colonel on. He'll I don't care who he's with!" These great lines gave colour to the movie and allowed Bruce Lee to develop his character in the film.

Although only a minor role, it was great in its own way, and it's thought that because of this role, he got another small acting part as a bank employee in That Man Bolt, a film that was made on the back of the success of the Enter The Dragon. Made by Universal Pictures, That Man Bolt starred Fred Williamson, a former football professional player in the NFL, who would go on to star with Jim Kelly in Three the Hard Way, Take A Hard Ride and One Down Three To Go. The film was trying to hit several genres including martial arts, blaxploitation and James

Bond-esque superspy films. The film also had help from one of Bruce's students Mike Stone and was fight choreographed by Emil Farkus, the martial artist who went on to stunt double the first Spiderman movies. It was released on 21st December 1973.

Geoffrey's only other claim to film fame was lending his voice to the English dub of Jimmy Wang Yu's *One-Armed Boxer* for Golden Harvest.

Sadly, Geoffrey Weeks passed away in late 1974, however, he would have known the success of *Enter The Dragon* and would have been proud of his contribution to film history.

Lee and Braithwaite share tea at the Shaolin Temple as they discuss the Lee's tournament entry.

Braithwaite and Lee view a reel of footage as they discuss Lee's mission on Han's island.

BETTY CHUNG
MAI LING - THE FEMALE SECRET AGENT

Betty Chung was born in 1947 in her ancestral hometown of Chengdu, Sichuan Province. In 1963, at the age of 16, she won a singing contest and moved to Hong Kong. From then on, she started to appear in various TV commercials and Hong Kong Television TVB shows including *Enjoy Yourself Tonight*. It was two years later in 1965 she had her film break in *The Lark* as a singer at a charity concert. On the back of her film roles, she was offered a record contract, which brought her a Chinese hit called *Go Go*. As a singer in both English and Mandarin, this dual-language skill would greatly benefit her success. Over the next two years, she had hits with *Bell A Go Go*, *Let's Pretend* and several others, which led to her second cameo movie appearance in *Incredible Rumour* (1968) as a singer in a club. Betty continued to have hit singles from 1968 to 1977, followed by a surprise revival in 2005.

From 1968, she had a steady stream of Hong Kong film appearances including *The Ruthless Heart* (1970), *Convivial Trio* (1970), *Song of a Happy Life* (1971) and *A Resort to Kill* (1972) .

However, her big break came when she appeared in *Enter the Dragon* as Mai Ling, the female operative sent to Han's Island by Mr Braithwaite in preparation for Lee's arrival as a guest of the martial arts tournament. Unfortunately, a lot of the great conversational dialog with Lee in his room and a great action fight scene choreographed by Bruce ended up on the cutting room floor, which is a shame as it helped the viewer of the film understand the storyline much better. However the editors said it slowed down the pace of this iconic martial arts action movie, which is the case with a lot of movies.

Betty only appeared in one more movie after *Enter the Dragon*. *All Men are Brothers* (aka *Seven Soldiers of Kung Fu*) released in 1975 by Shaw Brothers starred Betty as Li Shih-shih.

ENTER THE DRAGON

Bruce Lee choreographs a fight scene with Mai Ling (Betty Chung) and a guard.

Director Robert Clouse gives his instructions to Betty Chung and the smiling guard.

THE 50TH ANNIVERSARY COMPANION

The guard approaches Mai Ling as she preaperes her attack as the cameras roll.

Mai Ling's attack forces the guard backwards during filming of the scene.

ENTER THE DRAGON

The guard hits the floor after the strike from Mai Ling.

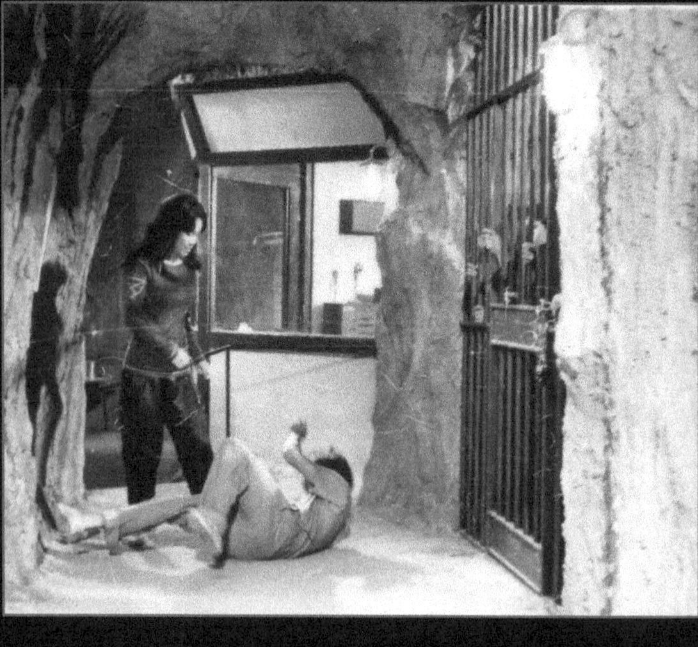

Mai Ling stands over the guard as the prisoners come to view the commotion.

Mai Ling stands over the guard as she prepares to free the prisoners.

Cinematographer Gil Hubbs frames Betty Chung's profile at the banquet.

The film also starred David Chiang (*Legend of the Seven Golden Vampires*), Bolo Yeung, Ti Lung, Michael Chan Wai-Man, Danny Lee (*Bruce Lee and I*) and a host of top Shaw Brother aartial arts stars of the 70s.

Miss Chung moved out of media limelight and only made a couple of TV appearances on *1st Hong Kong Gold Disc Award Presentation* and *The Miss Hong Kong Pageant*, both in 1977 and on the Hong Kong TVB network.

After these appearances, Chung left Hong Kong showbusiness scene in the 1980s and got married to the famous songwriter and music producer Chris Babida. However after a period of tim, the relationship ended in divorce.

She had one son and as far as is known resides somewhere in California. Her last known asurprise TV appearance was on a show called *Where Are They Now?* in 2006 for TVB.

Mai Ling (Betty Chung) blows the dart towards the apple at Han's banquet.

ROY CHIAO
THE SHAOLIN ABBOT

Roy Chiao was a Chinese actor born on 16th March 1927. In the 1970s, he was most famous for playing the Shaolin Abbot in *Enter the Dragon* (1973) and Billy Lo's Uncle in *Game of Death* (1978). In the 1980s, he was cast as the minor villain Lao Che in *Indiana Jones and the Temple of Doom* (1984) but it wasn't until 1988 that he would be remembered for one of most memorable roles as the formidable Sensei, Senzo Tanaka in the Jean-Claude Van Damme movie, *Bloodsport*.

In his time as an actor, he performed in many Hong Kong films with a career total of ninety films and also worked as an English language overdubber for Hong Kong produced films.

Outside of acting, Chiao was a United States Army interpreter during the Korean War.

He was the founder of "Artists' Home," a Christian Fellowship for actors in Hong Kong.

Throughout his life, he suffered three heart attacks before his heart disease-related death on 15th April 1999, aged 72.

His other film credits include *Ferry to Hong Kong* (1959) and *The Fate of Lee Khan* (1973).

Robert Clouse, Roy Chiao and Bruce Lee

TONY LIU
ROPER'S OPPONENT

Liu was born in 1952 in Hong Kong, where his mother, Li Wen, was a well-known actress. Liu studied at St. Paul's College, before going on to learn to play the piano at the Associated Board of the Royal Schools of Music (ABRSM). He practiced martial arts such as Judo, Kung Fu, Karate, and also learned Jeet Kune Do from Bruce Lee until Lee's death.

Liu joined the Hong Kong film production company, Golden Harvest in 1970, at the age of 18. He made his debut as the son of the villain in the 1971 film, *The Big Boss*, which starred Bruce Lee in his first major role. He also appeared in another three of Bruce Lee's films; as a martial arts student in *Fist of Fury* (1972); as a restaurant worker who practices Karate in *The Way of the Dragon* (1972); and as a tournament fighter who fights with John Saxon's character Roper in *Enter the Dragon* (1973). There was a rumour that Tony would also have had a part in Bruce's unfinished final film, *Game of Death*.

After Lee's death, he continued to make movies for Golden Harvest film, including *Naughty, Naughty* and *Seven Coffins*.

Tony Liu kicks John Saxon in rehearsals as Bruce Lee, Bob Wall and movie extras look on.

Bruce Lee choreographs John Saxon and Tony Liu in preparation for their fight scene

Studio in 1975 and made his first breakthrough role in *Emperor Chien Lung* (1976) its sequels. Liu also acted in several television shows produced by ATV.

Bruce Lee choreographs John Saxon and Tony Liu in preparation for their fight scene

PAT JOHNSON
"IT'S THE DOUGH, ROPER!"

Pat Johnson was born in 1939 in Niagara Falls, New York. He began training in traditional Korean Tang Soo Do Moo Duk Kwan in 1963, while stationed in South Korea as a chaplain in the U.S. Army. While under the tutelage of a Korean master named Kang Lo Hee, Johnson earned his black belt in just thirteen months. After his army service ended in 1968, Johnson met and formed an association with Tang Soo Do instructor Chuck Norris and soon rose to the rank of chief instructor at Norris' school in Sherman Oaks, California. That same year, he formulated the penalty-point system for use in Karate competitions, which is still used today.

From 1968 to 1973, Johnson was Captain of the undefeated Chuck Norris Black Belt Competition Team, which won thirty-three consecutive national and international titles. In 1971, he became the National Tang Soo Do Champion. In both 1975 and 1976, Johnson was awarded the prestigious Golden Fist

Bob Wall choreographs Pat Johnson as Robert Clouse directs.

Award for best Karate referee in the United States.

In 1973, Norris founded the National Tang Soo Do Congress (NTC), and named Johnson as executive vice president and chief of instruction. In 1979, Norris disbanded the NTC and formed the United Fighting Arts Federation (UFAF), again naming Johnson as executive vice president.

In that same year, Johnson had a memorable acting and choreography part in Enter the Dragon as Freddy's thug, who confronts Roper (John Saxon) on a golf course along with two other henchmen. Johnson had trained with Bruce Lee along with Chuck Norris and Bob Wall so between them, knew Bruce's vision for the film.

After Bruce's untimely death, Pat was easily persuaded to become involved in the film world and to capture the essence of what Bruce had started. His next martial arts stunt actor role was in the Jim Kelly movie Black Belt Jones (1974), followed by additional work on stunts with the team that had produced Enter the Dragon. These credits included Golden Needles (1974), The Ultimate Warrior (1975), and Hot Potato (1976).

He then went on to work with Chuck Norris on his fifth film project Good Guys Wear Black (1978) and co-wrote his sixth movie A Force of One (1979). He then did stunt work with his superstar student Steve McQueen on his last movie The Hunter in 1980.

Pat was then invited back by Robert Clouse to be the stunt coordinator on Jackie Chan's breakout Hollywood movie Battle Creek Brawl (1980) and followed by another of Clouse's martial arts epics Force: Five (1981) which starred all the top martial artists of that time including Joe Lewis, Ed Parker and Benny 'The Jet' Urquidez.

Johnson kept working on stunts, stunt coordinating and acting in films, however one of his most memorable roles came in 1984 with Johnson serving as stunt co-ordinator on Rocky director John G. Avildsen's The Karate Kid. Johnson also featured in the movie as the chief referee an the All Valley Karate Tournament. He was one of only four cast members who knew any martial arts before shooting began and therefore trained many of the cast for the movie.

In 1986, Johnson was promoted to ninth-degree black belt but after a difference of opinion with Chuck Norris, would leave the UFAF and reform the NTC. In this same year, he was welcomed back to serve as stunt co-ordinator for *The Karate Kid Part II* (1989) and with its continued success, it was no surprise that he would complete the trilogy with *The Karate Kid Part 3* in1989.

Due to his success as a stunt coordinator and working on *Enter the Dragon,* it was not difficult for Raymond Chow of Golden Harvest films to call Pat to be the stunt co-ordinator and choreographer for his new film *Teenage Mutant Ninja Turtles* in 1990, followed by its sequel *Teenage Mutant Ninja Turtles 2: The Secret of the Ooze* in 1991.

In the same year, Pat had the honour to work with Bruce Lee's son Brandon Lee on his third movie *Showdown In Little Tokyo* (1991) alongside Swedish action star Dolph Lundgren.

By now Pat was a very sought-after stunt co-ordinator and worked on the film version of *Buffy The Vampire Slayer* (1992), *Teenage Mutant Ninja Turtles* (1993), *The Next Karate Kid* (1994), *Mortal Kombat* (1995), *Mortal Kombat: Annihilation* (1997), *Batman & Robin* (1997), *Green Street Hooligans* (2005), and *Punisher: War Zone* (2008).

In 1995, he was credited as *Black Belt* magazine's Instructor of the Year.

Johnson's last known appearance was as an old man in a 2016 episode of a short-lived TV series based on the Jackie Chan's *Rush Hour*.

Sadly, as we celebrate the 50th year of *Enter the Dragon,* Pat has succumbed to the effects of Alzheimer's but his work and achievements are there fore everyone to see.

Roper grabs one of Freddy's hoods while Pat Johnson points a gun at the gambling man

YUEN WAH
THE MAN WHO MADE A DRAGON LOOK AMAZING

Yuen Wah was born Yung Chi on 9 September 1950 in Hong Kong. As a child, Yuan attended the China Drama Academy, a Peking Opera School in Hong Kong, where he was instructed by Master Yu Jim Yuen and became a member of the Seven Little Fortunes alongside fellow students including Jackie Chan, Sammo Hung, Yuen Biao, Yuen Qiu and Corey Yuen. Like the other students, he took his Sifu's given name – *Yuen*.

In his biography, Jackie Chan stated that Yuen Wah's martial arts ability was well respected among his fellow students, and after leaving the opera school, many of the students entered the Hong Kong film industry. Yuen Wah was given an anglicised stage name, Sam Yuen, but like Yuen Biao (Bill Yuen or Jimmy Yuen), the name was not used. Rather than reverting to their birth names, both retained their opera school names, as did several other former students. Like the other Fortunes, Wah's budding Peking Opera prospects did not survive as the popularity of the art declined.

From their mid-teens on, most of them had to become movie stuntmen - where thanks to the then surging martial art movie trend - there was plenty of work to be found for qualified daredevil acrobats. Eventually, Wah, along with many of his Peking Opera Academy brothers joined the Golden Harvest stunt team, headed by the Little Fortunes most senior member, big brother Sammo Hung.

Out of his entire fantastic Chinese movie career, the world should remember Yuen Wah as the man who truly made the late great Bruce Lee look amazing in *Enter the Dragon* and *Fist of Fury*.

As you are amazed by the martial arts skills and physical abilities of Bruce Lee in *Enter the Dragon*, there is something you should be made wise to. The fact that after Bruce injured his back some years before, his capability to do gymnastics was

Yuen Wah practices a somersault on an empty tennis court over Lee and an extra's raised arms.

limited and he was not going to do something that would injure his fledgling career such as performing spectacular tumbling somersaults, so someone else would have to perform them. Enter the unsung hero of two Bruce Lee films - Yuen Wah

Yuen Wah stood out from other stunt men right from the beginning due to his resourcefulness for acrobatic movements in addition to oulling off difficult technical execution. So it wasn't long before he was discovered and hired to act as a stuntman in scenes considered too risky or difficult for professional Kung Fu film actors.

After performing stunts and acting in six Shaw Brothers movies, Wah joined Golden Harvest just as they began preparation on the second movie by their newly-established Kung Fu superstar, Bruce Lee. In *Fist of Fury* (1972), a good dozen stuntmen were used as punching bags for the Little Dragon's fiery rage, most notably for the film's famed Japanese Karate dojo scene at the beginning of the film. Having the same body type as Bruce - wiry but muscular - Wah was also selected to be his designated acrobatic stunt-double. As fight scenes were staged on the spot, it was a wise move to have a stunt-double picked from the start. In the dojo scene, as Bruce Lee's character Chen Zhen squares off against the large-framed, spectacle-wearing Sensei, Yoshida (Yi Feng), and does a fantastic flip, it is not Lee, but Yuen Wah.

Yuen Wah himself appeared later on in the equally classic "No Dogs and Chinese allowed" park scene as a smirking Japanese man who tries to humiliate Chen at the entrance to the public cemetery and ends up receiving a beating, followed by a flying kick in an overwhelming sequence the Chinese audience went crazy about. When asked about this scene, he said in an interview, "I had ten years of Kung Fu training, so when I worked with Bruce Lee, the first time was in *Fist of Fury* and I played a young Japanese man. It was the part with the sign, 'No Dogs or Chinese Allowed.' I said, 'You want to go in? Only if you pretend you're a dog, then I'll walk you in like one.'"
"Then I got the shit kicked out of me by Bruce," he laughed.

Also in *Fist of Fury*, Wah ending up doubling Lee for a somersault he performs in Suzuki's office as he picks up the nunchakus to defend himself against the villain's samurai sword.

The following year, Wah was picked up again as a double

for Lee's fourth and final completed movie *Enter the Dragon*, this time for even more work. In the opening scene where Lee goes toe-to-toe with Sammo Hung, Bruce is present throughout, except where he executes a snap back-flip which was doubled by Yuen Wah. As Sammo advances against Lee with a series of rotating kicks, Lee - or rather, Yuen Wah with his back to the camera - throws himself backwards onto the floor before using his arms to propel himself back up to launch a snap punch to Hung's face. It is almost impossible to realise that it was not Bruce Lee performing the back-flip because their body type was so similar, since Bruce would had lost a lot of weight during the shooting of the movie.

After Lee has defeated Hung, the monks challenge him to jump over their raised arms. Lee smiles slightly, slaps his gloves and lets out a shout, performs several cartwheels and concludes with a spectacular acrobatic somersault over the monks' elevated arms. This was another amazing stunt performance not credited to Yuen Wah. These details about the film went unnoticed for many years and it was not until photographic proof revealed the true performer of these stunts. When Yuen was asked about this in an interview he replied, "The second time I worked with Bruce was during the making of *Enter the Dragon* where Bruce needed some tumbling movements. So they called me in to help out, and do some of these movements for him; it was as simple as that. Doing back flips for Bruce and any tumbling that needed him to bounce up right after being hit, those were the type of movements that I body doubled for him." Wah continued, "In *Enter the Dragon*, Bruce wanted to add some movements, so he wanted me to double for him and do a back flip, but he is the only one who knows how he actually wants it doing. So I think, 'What does he know and what style is it? Maybe a cartwheel! I know; I will double for him for the back flip.' So When I am flipping over the monks and over their raised arms in the black sleeves, I doubled for him there, passing over them, flipping and landing. Even his backside is me doubling Bruce, walking like this and swaggering." "Yes, I doubled Bruce Lee's backside walking too!" Wah said laughing.

Lee took advantage of Wah's ability in a few more scenes in *Enter the Dragon*. As an actor, he appears sitting and catching an apple with a dart thrown by one of Han's girls during the welcome banquet that preceded the martial arts tournament on

Lee and several extras watch Yuen Wah impressively somersault over them.

Bruce Lee's stunt double Yuen Wah, prepares for Oharra (Bob Wall) to grab his leg.

Bruce Lee's stunt double Yuen Wah, prepares for to kick Oharra (Bob Wall).

Oharra (Bob Wall) lets go of Yuen Wah's leg as he prepares to execute a somersault and kick.

the island.

Yuen Wah then appears in Han's drug caverns with a fake moustache as he emerges as one of the island's lookouts who tries to capture Lee during his exploration in the island's undergrounds caverns. Of course, Lee disposes of him extremely easily.

However, the most striking moment in *Enter the Dragon* that many believed was done by Bruce Lee, was actually performed perfectly by Yuen Wah, although he was not credited with this performance either. In the fight between Lee and the villain Oharra (Bob Wall), Lee hits him for the third time in the face and Oharra kneels due to the impact of the blow. Taking advantage of his position, Oharra tries to pull Lee's legs to bring it down desperately, but Lee throws himself into a spectacular back-flip kick, catching Oharra in the face on the way through. The person who performed the fantastic back-flip was Yuen Wah, again with his back to the camera. When asked about this in an interview he revealed, "Sometimes when I did these movements, Bruce also gave me his opinion. When you flip for example; after I had flipped, I have to kick, but he told me that while I was in mid-flip, I have to kick him. So my training for this movement was to flip, and kick at the same time, then land and stand. Originally, I was asked to do a flip, then a kick. After I flipped then kicked, Bruce said, 'No you kick while flipping. It has to be amazing.' So I said, 'Oh, oh, OK, I'll try it,' and one out of many takes, was OK."

Also, in *Enter the Dragon*, Wah also served as a fight extra being dealt with by Lee on more than one occasion. One of these occasions was when Lee does his super kick against Oharra. Yuen explains, "I remember a later scene when Bruce kicks Oharra back into the surrounding crowd and we had to use a shield of sand bags. Five of us had to withstand the power of his one side kicks, but then after he kicked, the five of us were like bowling pins ricocheting and bouncing in all directions."

Bruce Lee had many plans for the future. He intended to work in Hong Kong and produce his own films there and in the United States. One thing he was sure of; he would count on a first-rate stunt team, including great performers like Yuen Wah and Lam Ching-ying (*Mr Vampire*). Bruce had already penciled Yuen in for *Game of Death* but sadly never got to finish the movie so Yuen appeared in *Stoner*, Golden Harvest's schedule-replacing movie for *Game of Death*. Naturally, after Bruce Lee's sudden passing, it meant that both Lam and Wah stayed on as part of Golden Harvest's stunt crew.

Besides serving as a daredevil stuntman, Wah's remarkable set of physical abilities, together with his tall wiry frame, made him a valued stunt-double and fighting foil. He also had another asset going for him; his angular, weaselly face which he could easily shape into an intimidating mug or arrogant sneer. That's likely what got him his smirking Japanese role in *Fist of Fury*, as well as dozens of other tiny gigs over the years as thugs, henchmen and rowdy types that got into the hero's way and was trounced as a result. Between 1972 and 1977, Wah appeared, usually fleetingly, in nearly a dozen Golden Harvest productions including *Hap Ki Do*, *Back Alley Princess*, *None But the Brave*, *The Tournament*, *The Himalayan*, *Broken Oath*, *The Valiant Ones*, *Dragon Tamers*, and *Hand of Death*. Except for the first two of those movies, all action choreography was done by his former opera school classmate, Sammo Hung.

Most stuntmen spend a considerable amount of time developing new tricks to make themselves even more versatile and useful for the action directors who employed them. Wah's aforementioned mastery at martial arts forms meant that he was especially proficient at learning various types of Kung Fu and adapt them into savvy screen-fighting moves that were both graceful and spectacular, something which he could then use himself in movies or show to other stuntmen. His repertoire included, among others Eagle Claws, Taekwondo, Bak Mei and various sorts of Southern Fists techniques. In time, Wah came to adopt for himself a mixture of Taekwondo kicks and Eagle Claw techniques as his signature screen fighting style; an ingenious combo that wonderfully played not only with his aptitude in Kung Fu forms and acrobatics, but with his wiry framed and long spidery limbs and fingers as well. He also extensively practised with various sorts of weapon manoeuvres. Wah's phenomenal talents allowed him to quickly, even instantaneously, learn tricky acrobatic moves developed by other stuntmen as Wah himself revealed in an interview, "One of my friends trained secretly for about a week, to show me his one-handed back-flip. Normally such moves required two hands. He flipped using one hand, followed by a somersault in the air. I said, 'Is that all? I'll try and see if I can do it.' I push off and I did five flips at one go. 'You are not human,' the friend said, 'I'm not playing with you anymore.'"

Known for his agility and acrobatic skills, Yuen's versatility, and his distinctive moustache often saw him cast as the villain in most films. During the 1980s, he worked on several films with former classmates Jackie Chan, Sammo Hung and Yuen Biao, both in an action director and stunt co-ordinator capacity, as well as in acting roles as villainous characters. The films included *Mr. Vampire* (1985), *My Lucky Stars* (1985), *Millionaire's Express* (1986), *Eastern Condors* (1986), and *Dragons Forever* (1988).

During the 1990s, whilst still appearing in a number of films, Yuen began to focus on television series roles for TVB. In 1996, he starred as a Taoist Priest fighting vampires in the series, *The Night Journey*. His comical and endearingly scrooge-like image earned him popularity on the Hong Kong television circuit. Since then, he has appeared in over twenty different television series.

In 2004, Yuen was cast as The Landlord in Stephen Chow's action comedy film, *Kung Fu Hustle*, which also starred 1970s Bruceploitation star Bruce Leung as a major villain.

During the 2005 Hong Kong Film Awards, his colleagues took the opportunity to present him with the award for Best Supporting Actor.

Yuen made his English-language film debut in *Aiming High* (1998) and appeared in the Baz Luhrmann period film *Australia* (2008) another English-language production, starring Nicole Kidman and Hugh Jackman.

Yuen Wah (right) as the Landlord in Stephen Chow's 2004 action comedy *Kung Fu Hustle*.

ROBERT CLOUSE
DIRECTOR

Robert Clouse is best remembered for directing Bruce Lee in his iconic role in *Enter the Dragon* (1973). After Lee's death, Clouse finished Lee's incomplete film *Game of Death* and released it in 1978 with a new storyline and cast. Clouse was a writer and director, writing the screenplays for most of his films including Jim Kelly's *Black Belt Jones* (1974), *Golden Needles* (1974) starring Jim Kelly, *The Amsterdam Kill* (1977) starring Robert Mitchum, *Force: Five* (1981) starring Benny 'The Jet' Urquidez, Joe Lewis, Bong Soo Han and Richard Norton, *China O'Brien* (starring Cynthia Rothrock) (1990), Jackie Chan's US film debut *The Big Brawl* (1980), *Gymkata* (1985), *The Ultimate Warrior* (1975) and his last film, *Ironheart* (1992) starring Bolo Yeung. In 1984, he directed one episode of the TV show *The Master* starring Lee van Cleef, Sho Kosugi and Timothy Van Patten. Clouse also wrote two books; *Bruce Lee: The Biography*

Bruce Lee, Paul Heller and Robert Clouse on the Hall of Mirrors set.

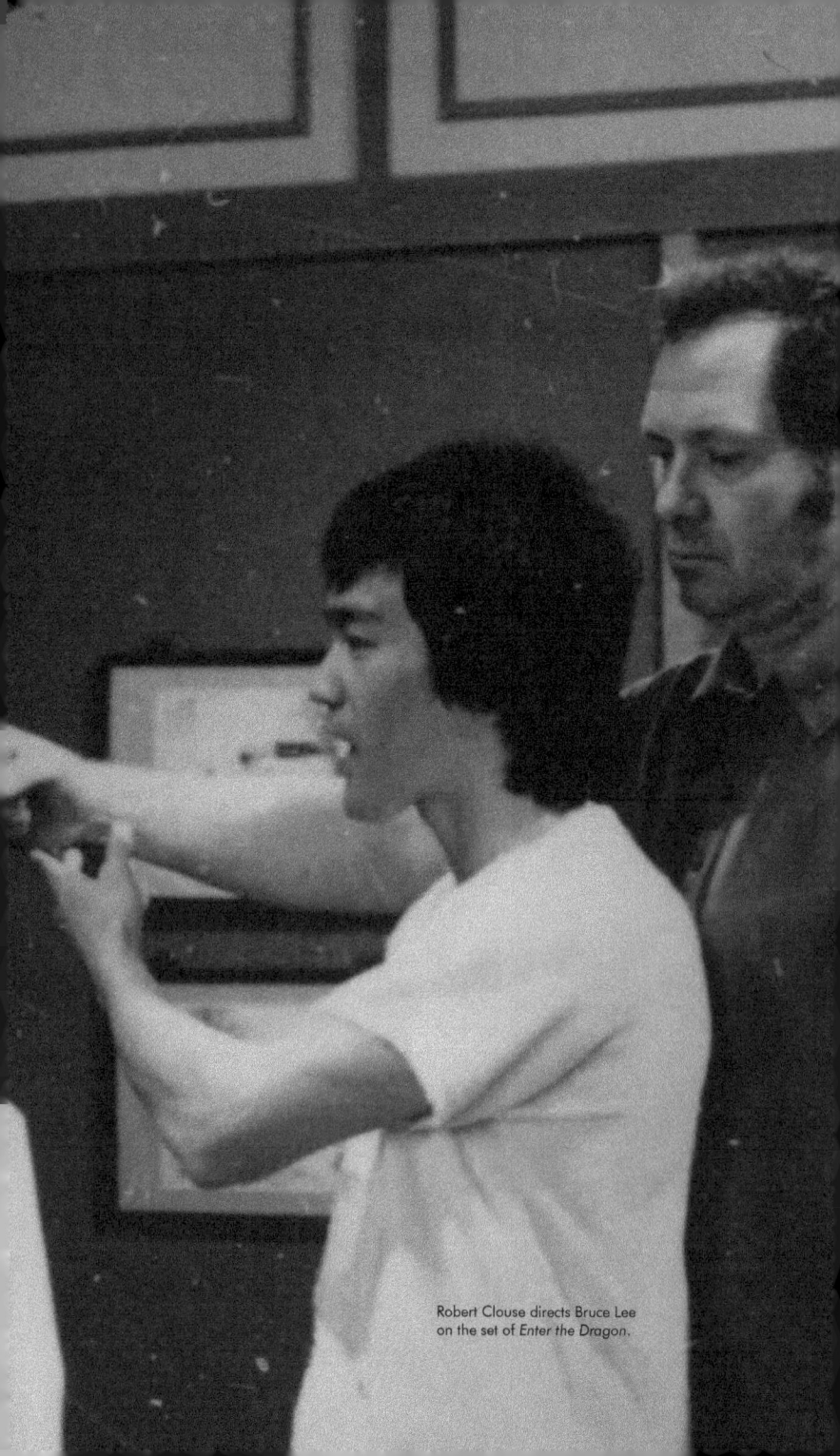

Robert Clouse directs Bruce Lee on the set of *Enter the Dragon*.

and *The Making of Enter the Dragon*, both released in 1989.

Released in 1970 was a little-known film called *Darker Than Amber*, an adaptation of a John D. MacDonald series of pulp novels. The story revolves around a tough guy - played by Hollywood bigshot of-the-time Rod Taylor - a brawny but sensitive salvage specialist in Florida who deals with murder and lost love. In the show, he he has a blood-curdling and brilliantly rendered fight. against a terrifying villain played by William Smith, who auditioned for Kwai Chang Caine in the television series, *Kung Fu*.

When it came for Bruce Lee to choose a director for his Hollywood breakthrough *Enter the Dragon*, Bruce remembered this fantastic fight scene, and how it was filmed; showing all the action with both hands and feet which was something most Hollywood directors have a problem with and insist on cutting in on the action instead of showing the full fight action, in direct contrast to Hong Kong Kung Fu action movies. For this reason, he picked Robert Clouse to direct and so the partnership began.

Another element that was brought from this film was sultry actress Ahna Capri, who had starred in this movie. Due to her beauty, she was cast as Han's Dragon Madam in *Enter the Dragon* on the back of Clouse's suggestion. Rod Taylor was also originally considered for the role of Roper, but he was thought to be too tall in comparison to Bruce Lee, with whom he was to share many action scenes.

Although Bruce had been impressed by Clouse's movie directing capabilities, Lee insisted that the two of them go out together to a movie theatre to watch one of his movies on his first night in Hong Kong in January 1973. Lee told Clouse that he wanted him to experience the atmosphere, but the real reason was that when they first met, Clouse was completely unaware of Lee's reputation. Although the outing was to impress Clouse, it was also to psych Lee up for the production.

Even at this stage of production, Lee was concerned about the character he was portraying in *Enter the Dragon*; He was very unsure whether the west would accept a Chinese hero and whether the Chinese would accept his new approach.

Unfortunately, Clouse did not turn out to be what Bruce expected and so they started to have a constant directorial battle on the set of the first major martial arts movie ever made, that by the standards of Lee's other films, had a huge budget, and the reality was, he was not going to blow it. From then on, there was a lot of friction between the two of them.

Clouse had no respect for martial arts action people; he only had respect for actors, so he was only nice to the 'stars' on the movie, but he wasn't nice to the star of that movie, Bruce Lee. For example, Clouse was very nice to John Saxon and Ahna Capri because they were an 'actors,' however, he was not nice to Bruce Lee, Bob Wall or any other martial artist on the set and it was irrelevant to him how many Hong Kong movies they had starred in.

With a turn of fate, the unthinkable happened on 20th July 1973 as Bruce Lee died of a cerebral oedema at the age of 32 and only days before *Enter the Dragon* got its official theatrical release. Lee never got to enjoy his biggest success, as *Enter the Dragon* was released six days after his death. The film went on to gross an estimated US$350 million worldwide (equivalent to more than US$1 billion today, adjusted for inflation), against a production budget of US$850,000, making it the most profitable martial arts film ever.

It was not down to Robert Clouse's directorial skills that made the film a phenomenon, but Lee's screen presence and exquisite movement, which was unlike anyone else. Through reimagining the martial arts, Bruce Lee brought the western world arguably the greatest Kung Fu movie ever made in *Enter the Dragon*.

Like all of the movies he ever filmed, it was all about him. A lot of the footage was solely to bookend his transformative fight scenes. When Lee paused for a split second in one of his usual stances, idiosyncratically twitching and striking poses, you knew a bust-out was imminent. The entire audience stopped to watch, however, and whenever Lee's mighty nunchakus dominated the scenes, the exhibition exploded onto the screen. The cameras were too slow to catch their action and so the whole audience would be in awe and amazement at the skill and precision. Their use easily became a trademark of all his movies due to their popularity. Also, another trademark of Bruce's was his war cries during the fight sequences. All of these elements and more made this an iconic picture, which it what it remains to this day.

As soon as Bruce had passed away, the box office takings

confirmed an urgent void for martial arts movies has been left.

Warner Brothers quickly signed up Jim Kelly to a three-picture deal and wanted the same team and formula that had been so successful at creating the right vehicle for Bruce Lee in *Enter the Dragon*. Just about everyone who had been involved in Lee's first Hollywood outing was brought back for *Black Belt Jones*, including direct Robert Clouse. Released on 28th March 1974, *Black Belt Jones* saw yet again Clouse ruffling the feathers of the martial artists in this movie, including his main star Jim Kelly as well as Bob Wall, who never really forgave him for his actions towards the 'non-actors' of *Enter the Dragon*, as he called them. The film had a modicum of success, mainly due to the catch line, "From The Team That Brought You *Enter the Dragon*."

As Bob Wall would say bitterly, "No one knew Robert Clouse before *Enter the Dragon*." However, Clouse was smart, and he quickly saw that, after Bruce had died, he had become a world phenomenon and in fact had exposed the west to a new film genre. With help and blessing of Warner Brothers and the Lee family, mainly Linda Lee, he set about writing a script for a biopic on Bruce Lee's life based on Linda's first biography on her husband's life called, *Bruce Lee: The Man I Only Knew*. So, by 26th March 1975 Clouse delivered a final draft of the script to Warner Brothers for *Bruce Lee: His Life and Legend*.

The search for a new Bruce Lee had begun. Unfortunately the film never got made because Stanley Kubrick's movie *Barry Lyndon* ran over budget and producers Barbra Streisand and Jon Peters took their money to plough it into *A Star is Born*, winning several awards, including a Golden Globe for Best Motion Picture (Music or Comedy) in the process.

Due of his history with Bruce Lee, Clouse was called upon to finish Lee's incomplete film *Game of Death*, which was released in 1978 with a new storyline and cast.

In 1993, Clouse received a partial writing credit for the script to *Dragon: The Bruce Lee Story* due to the influence of his *Bruce Lee: His Life and Legend* script and his book, *Bruce Lee: The Biography*.

Overall, Robert Clouse did very well out of his affiliation with Bruce Lee and *Enter the Dragon*.

Robert Clouse died of kidney failure on 4th February 1997 in Ashland, Oregon at the age of 68.

Bruce Lee, Gil Hubbs, Robert Clouse and the camera crew discuss shooting on the Hall of Mirrors set.

Robert Clouse positions Han's bladed hand in the Trophy Room.

Bruce Lee shares one of few light-hearted moments with Robert Clouse in a break from filming.

FRED WEINTRAUB
PRODUCER

Fred Weintraub was an American film and television producer well known for the first martial arts film *Enter the Dragon*, starring Bruce Lee. Defying the film industry's prejudices, he created a worldwide phenomenon by bringing the first third-world superstar, Bruce Lee, into the mainstream and thus began the martial arts craze around the world. Weintraub produced many martial arts movies including *Black Belt Jones, Golden Needles, Hot Potato, Jaguar Lives, Battle Creek Brawl, Force Five, Gymkata, China O'Brien* and its *sequel China O'Brien 2* as well as directing the 1993 Bruce Lee documentary, *Curse of the Dragon*. He also served as a producer on *The Best of Martial Arts*, a martial arts movie compilation documentary narrated by John Saxon.

Bruce Lee and Fred Weintraub on the tournament grounds set.

PAUL HELLER
PRODUCER

Paul Heller was an American film producer, residing in Southern California. His debut as a film producer was *David and Lisa*, which received two Oscar nominations. He was the executive producer of 1990's Oscar winner *My Left Foot*, which earned five Academy Award nominations for Best Actor and Best Supporting Actress. Heller worked as a Warner Bros. executive, overseeing such films as *Skin Game*, starring James Garner, and *Dirty Harry*, starring Clint Eastwood.

In 1973, Heller founded Sequoia Pictures, Inc., a production house affiliated with Warner Bros. The company's first production was *Enter the Dragon*, the film that spurred interest in the martial arts genre and which introduced Bruce Lee to the international film market. Mr. Heller also had a cameo part in *Enter The Dragon* as the operator who receives a message from Lee, telling them to send help and get him off Han's Island. After Lee's untimely death in the same year that *Enter the Dragon* was released Paul, went on to make several other martial arts

Bruce Lee and Paul Heller on the *Enter the Dragon* set.

films for Warner Brothers including *Black Belt Jones* (1974) with Jim Kelly, *The Ultimate Warrior* (1975) with Yul Bruner and *Hot Potato* (1976) again with Jim Kelly. He then he had a run of cult mainstream movie hits like *Withnail & I* (1987) and *My Left Foot: The Story of Christy Brown* (1989).

Bruce Lee, Paul Heller and Robert Clouse have fun on the radio room set.

Paul Heller shows Bruce Lee how to use Morse Code on the radio room set.

His last noted short documentary film was *Blood and Steel: The Making of Enter the Dragon* in 2003. Although he has gone, you can still hear the sense of pride he held for *Enter the Dragon* from his passionate audio commentary featured on the later Warner Brothers' home media releases of the film.

RAYMOND CHOW
THE MAN WHO HELPED CREATE A DRAGON

The legendary Hong Kong film producer, Raymond Chow was born in Hong Kong on October 8th 1927. He attended St. John's University in Shanghai before returning to Hong Kong in 1949, where he worked as a newspaper reporter before working as a radio and television producer for a number of years. In 1958, Shaw Brothers recruited him as a publicist, becoming head of the studio's production department.

Raymond Chow became frustrated at the Shaw Brothers studio's ethic of churning out hundreds of low-budget Kung Fu and swordplay films. Although he could have stayed a top executive at Shaw Brothers, he was not happy with the quality of the studio's output (also in part due to another matter involving the promotion of someone in the company), so left in 1970 to create his own production company, Golden Harvest. Initially, Golden Harvest films did poorly, but Raymond Chow's company went on to have a very successful run, producing more than six hundred films in a range of genres and in the process, Raymond Chow nurtured a number of international superstars and directors.

Shaw Brothers previously had a monopoly over the market but Golden Harvest led Hong Kong box-office sales in the 1970s and 1980s.

Golden Harvest produced several American box-office hits, including *The Cannonball Run*, which had an all-star cast headed by Burt Reynolds. Through this film, Chow hoped to develop the market in the US for Jackie Chan and Michael Hui, both of whom had roles in the film. The previous year, Chow had introduced Jackie Chan to Western audiences in *The Big Brawl* (1980), and the two of them went on to make a number of Chinese language films together, making Chan a huge star in Asia. Indeed, Raymond Chow introduced many Hong Kong actors to international audiences, contributing to the development

ENTER THE DRAGON

of the Hong Kong film industry.

It was Jackie Chan's 1995 collaboration with Raymond Chow, *Rumble in the Bronx*, which brought Jackie Chan worldwide fame. In 2000, Jackie Chan told *Variety*, "Mr. Chow gave me a chance to follow my dreams. I think today that without Golden Harvest, there is no Jackie Chan."

Raymond Chow produced the Hollywood-made big screen adaptations of *Teenage Mutant Ninja Turtles*, which were also very successful. The first film took in more than $200 million

Bruce Lee and Raymond Chow outside Golden Harvest studios.

alone.

In 1998, Raymond Chow was awarded the Gold Bauhinia Star medal, Hong Kong's highest honour for his contribution to the local film industry.

Golden Harvest made its last film in 2003, with Raymond Chow officially announcing his retirement in Hong Kong on 5th November 2007. He sold his stake in Golden Harvest to Chinese businessman Wu Kebo, who merged it with his own

entertainment group to create Orange Sky Golden Harvest Entertainment.

In 2008 at the age of 81, Raymond Chow received the Lifetime Achievement Award at the Hong Kong Film Awards.

The Raymond Chow/Golden Harvest story may not have been one of success if it was not for one man - Bruce Lee. While Bruce Lee visited Hong Kong from 27th March to 16th April 1970 to make arrangements for his mother, Grace, and his brother, Robert, to take up residency in the US, Unicorn Chan (Siu Kee Lun) approached the head of Shaw Brothers, Run Run Shaw, on Bruce Lee's behalf, with instructions regarding a potential film offer; to make one film for the studio for a fee of US$10,000.

Raymond Chow, Andre Morgan, Dave Friedman, John Saxon and Bruce Lee outside Golden Harvest studios.

Bruce Lee also attached other conditions and additions. By the time Shaw Brothers replied to Bruce Lee's offer, he was back in the US. Run Run Shaw's proposal was a seven-year contract for $2,000 a film, which Bruce Lee refused to accept.

In 1970, Raymond Chow told *Forbes*, "When you are fortunate, you try to take advantage. And when you get a bad hand, you just try to watch yourself, maximise your losses so that you don't get killed."

In 1971, Raymond Chow sent one of his producers Liu Liang-hua - the wife of director Lo Wei - to Los Angeles with the intention of getting Bruce Lee to sign a film contract. Golden Harvest was facing financial difficulties at this time and was close to being made bankrupt. Raymond Chow recognised Bruce Lee's skills and star quality, having seen his impressive performance on the Hong Kong television show *Enjoy Yourself Tonight*, where Bruce Lee did a

board-breaking display.

Also, according to Hong Kong media reports, Raymond Chow heard a radio interview whereby Bruce Lee responded to a question asking if he would do a film in Asia, with the reply, "If the price is right....." As well as that, *The Green Hornet* television series had been renamed *The Kato Show* in Hong Kong, due to the popularity of Bruce Lee's character. Raymond Chow believed Bruce Lee could change the flailing fortunes of Golden Harvest - and he was right!

On 28th June 1971, Bruce Lee signed a two-picture deal

with Golden Harvest - to do two films for a fee of US$15,000, along with a say in the production and a share of the profits. Those two films became *The Big Boss* and *Fist of Fury*.

When Run Run Shaw discovered Bruce Lee had decided to do two films for Golden Harvest, he made an improved offer, but Bruce Lee had already signed the contract and was an honourable man.

The Big Boss, filmed in Thailand in 1971, became the most successful film shown in Hong Kong up to that point, breaking

Andre Morgan, John Saxon, Raymond Chow and Bruce Lee outside Golden Harvest studios.

Raymond Chow looks on as Bruce Lee holds out a side kick as he prepares to tell Oharra, "Outside!"

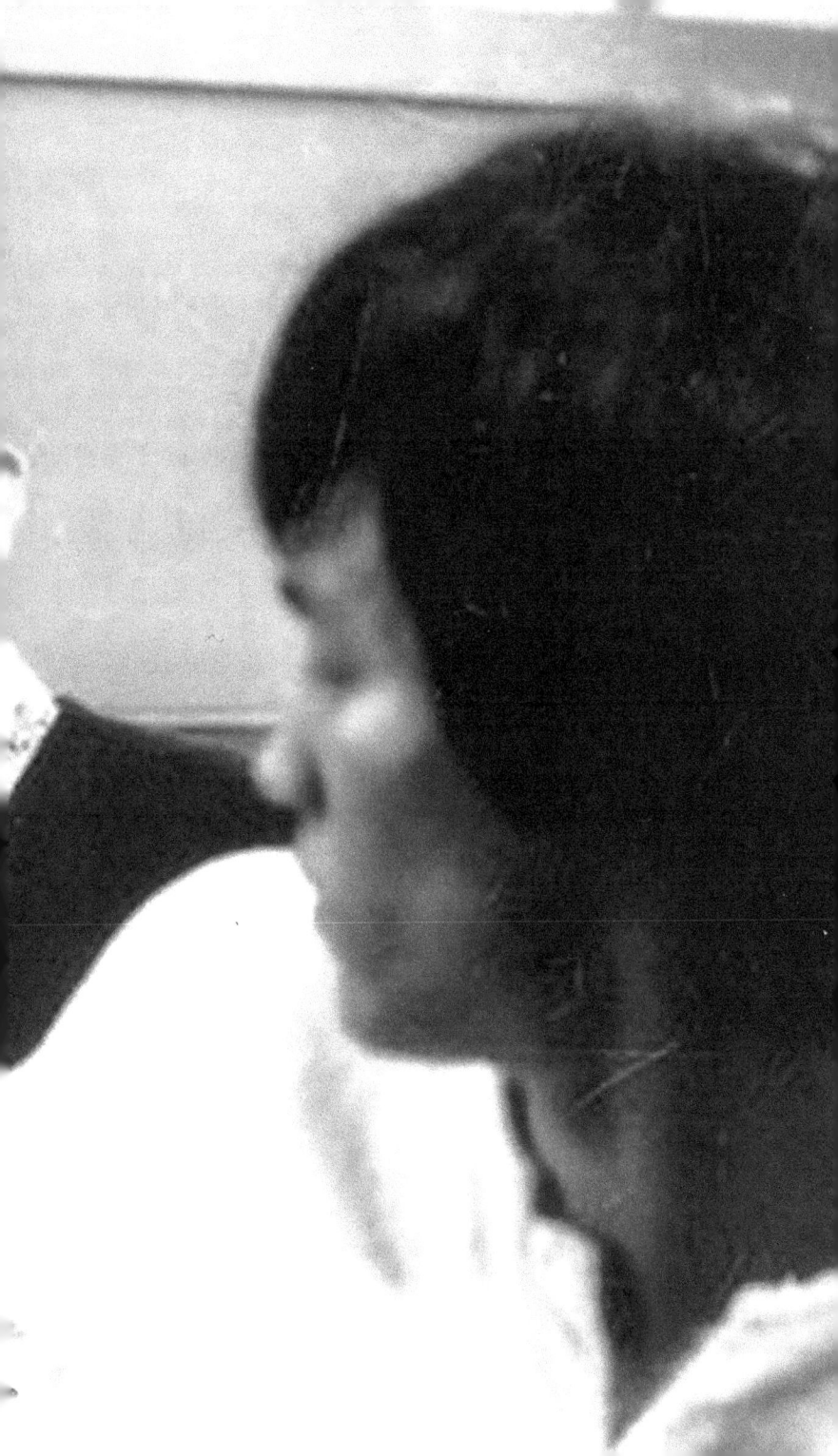

all box office records – and ensuring the survival of Golden Harvest. *Fist of Fury* quickly followed and broke all the previous records set by *The Big Boss*.

It has been widely documented that Bruce Lee and Raymond Chow became partners and formed Concord Production after the release and success of *Fist of Fury* in March 1972, but Bruce Lee and Raymond Chow signed the contract establishing a new company in December 1971.

Bruce Lee wrote in a letter to Ted Ashley (the Chairman of Warner Brothers films and occasional student of his) dated 16th December 1971, "...I have started a film company (Concord) with a trusted friend of mine, and am looking forward very much to work with Warner on some future projects..."

After the release of Bruce Lee's second film *Fist of Fury* in 1972, Warner Brothers' Production Executive, Fred Weintraub flew to Hong Kong, eager to strike a movie deal with Bruce Lee and Raymond Chow. Fred Weintraub and Paul Heller were co-producers of a subsidiary company, Sequoia, set up to manage the project, with the idea being for Sequoia and Concord to co-produce the film. Fred Weintraub recalled, "Even as I boarded the flight to Hong Kong, I knew I was in for a hell of a fight. Raymond Chow had a lot invested in Bruce and would be very protective of his cash cow."

Fred Weintraub later commented, "One thing we both knew was that action movies make most of their money on foreign distribution, so dividing the territories was going to be the most contentious part of the negotiation. I had negotiated my share of deals and I could be tricky. However, Raymond Chow was smart. He knew he had the bargaining advantage because Bruce was under contract to Golden Harvest and was already making a ton of money for them. And since Raymond was well aware that American stardom was Bruce's holy grail, the only way he could be sure to keep Bruce for himself was to block the production by making unreasonable demands. So Raymond Chow asked for the world. It was obvious he did not want the deal to go through, so he kept insisting on more and key foreign territories, knowing I could not give them up. He did not want to alienate his star, so he kept up the pretence of bargaining in good faith; when the deal fell through, he could assure Bruce that it was the American's fault. In the spirit of moving forward, I gave Raymond Chow almost everything he asked for. And he still said no."

Things worked out for Fred Weintraub when he told Bruce Lee, in front of Raymond Chow, "I'm leaving tomorrow because we couldn't strike a deal. I am sorry things did not work out. It's too bad Raymond doesn't want you to be an international star." This prompted Bruce Lee to say, "Sign the contract, Raymond."

Fred Weintraub boarded the plane the next day with a signed contract in his pocket, however, he still had to get Warner Brothers to accept the new terms and negotiations would later continue. Fred Weintraub was unsure Warner Brothers would approve the new Bruce Lee deal.

In March 1972, shortly before filming began on Bruce Lee's and Raymond Chow's next film, *The Way of the Dragon*, Bruce Lee and his wife, Linda were accompanied by Raymond Chow in the foyer at the Hyatt Regency hotel in Hong Kong after finishing a meal to celebrate Linda's birthday, when they met former Shaw Brothers actress, Betty Ting Pei. Raymond Chow introduced Bruce Lee and Betty Ting Pei to one another. Betty Ting Pei would go on to play a significant role in Bruce Lee's life - and death.

The Way of the Dragon, which Lee not only starred in and produced, but also directed in his directorial debut, it completely smashed the records set by *The Big Boss* and *Fist of Fury*.

Immediately after the completion of *The Way of the Dragon* in August 1972, Bruce Lee began working on his next film, *The Game of Death*. In September 1972, Bruce Lee visited Shaw Brothers where he met director Corey Yuen and several of the actors.

Filming of *The Game of Death* was halted when Bruce Lee and Raymond Chow flew to Los Angeles on 29th October 1972 to finalise the deal with Warner Brothers. *Enter the Dragon* would become the first co-production between Hong Kong and Hollywood, ultimately becoming a film that would make a phenomenal impact all over the world.

When Fred Weintraub went to Hong Kong prior to the LA trip, it was difficult for him to get Bruce Lee and Raymond Chow in the same room as he seemed to think that Raymond Chow felt that he was losing control. If Raymond Chow thought that, then what must he have been thinking and feeling when Bruce Lee had a period costume test photo shoot at the Shaw Brothers' studios in April 1973?

Bruce Lee, Raymond Chow and Paul Heller on the Shaolin Temple Abbot set.

Bruce Lee plays around with Raymond Chow on the Trophy Room set.

It has been reported that Bruce Lee did not intend to sign a contract with Shaw Brothers and that it was just a plan to deliver a message to Raymond Chow. However, contrary to these reports, Bruce Lee indicated that he was intending to do a film with Shaw Brothers when, in a letter to Run Run Shaw, he later wrote, "As of now, consider September, October and November - a period of three months, reserved for Shaw."

There were reports that Bruce Lee and Raymond Chow's relationship became strained, to the point that they had arguments and disagreements over several issues; especially those relating to the accounting for *The Way of the Dragon*.

On Friday 20th July 1973, Bruce Lee typed a letter to his lawyer Adrian Marshall in Los Angeles. The letter included working out a tax plan and the listing of four deals to be between Adrian Marshall and himself. Interestingly, Bruce Lee typed, "...I would like to meet with you first before meeting with Raymond Chow and then both of us will hear him out..." Bruce Lee also added, "...I won't sign anything until I and then maybe Raymond Chow and/or SY sit down and we all talked..."

Later, on the evening of 20th July 1973, Raymond Chow and former James Bond star, George Lazenby, waited for Bruce Lee and Betty Ting Pei to join them at the Miramar hotel restaurant, where aspects of The Game of Death - which Lee was pre-

Bruce Lee and Raymond Chow in discussion on the tournament set.

paring to resume filming after taking time out to shoot *Enter the Dragon* - were going to be discussed, but Bruce Lee and Betty Ting Pei never turned up. While at Betty Ting Pei's apartment, Bruce Lee was taken ill. After receiving a phone call from Betty Ting Pei, Raymond Chow drove to her apartment and an ambulance was called, following much delay due to Chow trying to revive Lee, before conceding defeat and calling for a doctor.

A report stated, "Ambulance number 43 received a call at 22:30 hours on Friday July 20 at number 67 Beacon Hill Road....taken to Queen Elizabeth Hospital...arrived at 23:00 hours that night."

Bruce Lee's wife, Linda arrived at the hospital before the ambulance. Bruce Lee was unconscious when he was rushed into the hospital and he never regained consciousness.

After Bruce Lee's death, *The Game of Death* footage that Bruce Lee had shot was placed into storage in the Golden Harvest vaults. The rights to that footage automatically became the property of the Bruce Lee estate and his widow, Linda. Raymond Chow bought out those rights and in 1978 produced a version of *The Game of Death* - dropping *The* from the title inn the process - that only contained eleven minutes of Bruce Lee's original footage. Even so, *Game of Death* beat Bruce Lee's previous box office records. Great business!

The first Bruce Lee documentary was Golden Harvest's *Bruce Lee: The Man and the Legend*, filmed by Raymond Chow only a few days after Lee's death in order to cash in on his deceased star. It was shown in Hong Kong cinemas in late 1973 and includes footage inside Bruce Lee's home in Kowloon and of his memorial service held on 25th July 1973.

The film was then withdrawn from circulation. Later, in the 1980s, Raymond Chow created an updated version of the documentary and released it as *Bruce Lee: The Legend*.

Raymond Chow, the 'Godfather' of Hong Kong films, passed away, aged 91 on 2nd November 2018. He will be remembered for being the man who catapulted Bruce Lee onto the international stage, leading to Bruce Lee becoming a cultural icon.

Following Chow's death, Bruce Lee's daughter, Shannon, paid tribute to Raymond Chow when she posted, "Thank you Raymond for taking a chance on a young Bruce Lee and helping him to realize his dream. Rest in peace, Raymond."

ANDRE MORGAN
ASSOCIATE PRODUCER

Andre Morgan was born in French Morocco as an only child to an American who served in the Navy, and an English mother. Raised as a Navy Brat, Andre spent most of his childhood in different cities in both Europe and America. By by the time he was sixteen, he had been enrolled in twelve elementary and junior high schools. This exposure to many different cultures peaked his interest in the history of other cultures, however it was not until college that he began to learn anything about Asian cultures.

Deciding to pursue degrees in Oriental languages, Chinese History and Asian studies was more a matter luck than design. Andre Morgan needed scholarships to stay in college, and the only ones available were in these fields. He joined the Department of Oriental Languages and Literature at the University of Kansas, majoring in Chinese and getting a draft deferment that kept him out of the Vietnam War. He had a passion for the film industry and wanted to go to Hong Kong to improve his Chinese.

In Hong Kong, he got a job with Raymond Chow's film production company Golden Harvest because the head of the Chinese department at Kansas had been a close friend of Chow's in the late 1940s. They'd set up Voice of America in Hong Kong together. When he told his professor he wanted to go to Asia, he said he'd make a few phone calls and see if there were any jobs available. Raymond Chow had formed Golden Harvest five months previous and they made a pact that if he was to come out and spend a year in Hong Kong, working for a local Chinese salary, he'd give him a job as an office boy.

He met Bruce Lee on his second day in Hong Kong and they were the only two Americans in the company. Before he got to Hong Kong, he didn't know Bruce Lee from any other actor. He had a vague recollection of having seen him in a couple

ENTER THE DRAGON

Bruce Lee, Raymond Chow, Dave Friedman and Andre Morgan outside Golden Harvest studios.

episodes of *The Green Hornet* and in a cameo appearance in an episode of *Ironside* with Raymond Burr. But when he arrived, they sat him down and, before he met Bruce Lee, he watched his first two movies, *The Big Boss* and *Fist of Fury*.

By helping the production team make movies that would be more marketable to western markets, Morgan was promoted from office boy to producer within three months of arriving in Hong Kong.

Mr. Morgan had observed a lot of differences in the martial

arts film industry since he began working in it in the early 1970s. He began working with Bruce Lee, whose own personal style went on to inspire a whole generation of martial arts actors. The industry began to move away from over the top performances and became more reality based, more grounded and less theatrical. Flying kicks and cases of twenty men attacking one became less and less common as time went on.

Andre went on to help *Enter the Dragon* become the success it has become today and worked on most Golden Harvest Productions including Bruce Lee's *Game of Death* (1978) and the *Cannonball Run* series of films , as well as appearing in a few of the films like *When Tae Kwon Do Strikes* and *The Man from Hong Kong*.

He stayed in Hong Kong until 1985. He started as an office boy and by the time he left, he was running the largest division in the largest film company in Asia. They had offices in London and Los Angeles. They had a huge theatre system to distribute their English-language and Chinese pictures.

He partnered up with Al Ruddy after getting to know him when he worked with Golden Harvest on the *Cannonball Run* movies and set up Ruddy-Morgan together. They produced *The Warlords* (2007) and created the American television show *Martial Law* for established Hong Kong star Sammo Hung.

MICHAEL ALLIN
SCRIPT WRITER

Michael Allin was born in 1944 and is best-known for writing the film script to Enter the Dragon, the 1973 smash hit that launched the western career for martial arts star, Bruce Lee. Unfortunately it was Lee's last film, as he died on the 20th July - a week before its world premiere in Hollywood. After writing Enter the Dragon, Allin wrote or helped to write the screenplays for several other films including Blaxploitation film Truck Turner (1974) starring musician Isaac Hayes, Nichelle Nichols of the Star Trek fame and Yaphet Kotto of Alien and Live and Let Die fame.

One of Allin's other great film script collaborations was the 1980s film adaptation based on the early film serial of Flash Gordon, which was a great success, as well as launching the film career of former American football player Sam J. Jones. He also worked on the film scripts for Hotel Paradise (1995) and I'll Be Home for Christmas (1998).

Aside from writing film scripts Allin's literary debut was 1998's Zarafa: A Giraffe's True Story, from Deep in Africa to the Heart of Paris. This first book took a complete change of subject matter from his film work. Critics were much more generous with their praise of Zarafa than of Allin's previous writings.

Allin also made appearances in the 2004 documentary Blood and Steel: The Making of Enter the Dragon and the 2020 documentary Lost in Space: Nicolas Roeg's Flash Gordon.

Allin currently resides in San Diego and makes public talks about his career and his links to Enter the Dragon.

At a recent 2023 TCM classic Film Festival celebrating the 50th anniversary of Enter the Dragon with a screening in Los Angeles, he was asked how he got involved with the movie and he replied:

"I was a punk kid, was 28 years old, had friends which I

had written various attempts at scripts and I had a friend who believed in me. His partner was Fred Weintraub, who had a relationship with Bruce Lee, who said to me, 'If you come up with something for me, I will do it,' because by then, he had become a big star in Hong Kong and they asked me to write it. It took three weeks to write and I was so excited. What happened was that we watched all of Bruce's movies and I got to Warner Bothers on the lot to go to the screening room and watching. I felt like movie trash. We watched everything and that was the research so then I went away, wrote the script and Bruce said, 'Yes' to it. However, the really interesting thing was the movie business does not usually work that way; it takes years and years and contacts like Travolta says, 'No,' and Richard Gere says, 'Yes,' and it usually goes on forever. From treatment to finishing *Enter the Dragon*, it was four months and was because, number one - it was so economically done for US$875,000 including prints and advertising. Secondly, Bruce just amazed everybody; he had no character and all the other actors characters are there to back him up as Warners would not believe in an Asian actor. They had already broken his heart about *Kung Fu* by giving the lead part to David Carradine and that had been Fred Weintraub's project too, and they would not go with Bruce, so all of a sudden, you turn the camera on Bruce Lee and oh my god, what he did without a character. What Bruce was about and all the MMA stuff about fighting. His really great thing was the art of fighting without fighting, and in the fifty years since the movie came out, think of all the non-contact arts that have come from this philosophy. Bruce was a teacher; that's who he really, really was and what

happened with Bruce, is that he wanted to be a movie celebrity and his students were movie stars, so he evolved in that direction and forgive me for saying this, but that his tension in his personality, was that he was an angel in his expertise but his career desire was elsewhere.

Bruce was really happy when Lalo Schifrin did the music because his great workout music was the theme from the *Mission Impossible* TV series. He worked out to that theme exclusively. Nobody made more money on that show than Lalo Schifrin.

Years Later I was taking to a Japanese lawyer at Warner Brothers studios, he was a grown man and he said, 'You and Bruce Lee saved my life!' So I said, 'Why? What happened?' He said, 'I was seven years old; I was a little wimpy Japanese kid going to elementary school picked on, bullied, whatever. *Enter the Dragon* comes out and all I have to do is assume the stance and make the scream and they ran for their lives.

That's the power of Bruce Lee and Enter the Dragon and so it shall remain so."

GILBERT HUBBS
CINEMATOGRAPHER

Gilbert 'Gil' Hubbs was born on 22nd January 1942 and not much is known about his personal life. However, he has a been working as a cinematographer in Los Angeles since 1965, shooting documentaries, commercials, television programs and features. The film he is best associate with is *Enter the Dragon*.

Working on this job was not the easiest as Gill joined the Hong Kong-based production late in preparation and Hubbs had never shot a feature on 35mm before, which was unbeknown to Robert Clouse. Hubbs was also required to shoot the picture in anamorphic widescreen. Unimpressed with the optics available from the studio camera department, he tracked down a set of Panavision lenses at a local Hong Kong rental house and managed to film the entire movie using two Arriflex cameras with only three Panavision lenses. However he was shocked at how little care and expense went into the minutiae of the Hong Kong production system, from the camera equipment to the film processing lab. Due to Gil's fluid photography, it made interesting, widescreen photography and introduced the west to many handsome Hong Kong locations and Hubb's garish photography was entirely appropriate for this movie.

After *Enter the Dragon*, he worked on many film and TV productions, with the most memorable of these being *Golden Needles* (1974) with Joe Don Baker and Jim Kelly and *Flowers in the Attic* (1987) where he was director of photography. He also appeared in the Bruce Lee documentaries *On Location: Hong Kong with Enter the Dragon* (1973) *The Path of the Dragon* (1998) and *Blood and Steel: The Making of Enter the Dragon* (2004). Hubbs has appeared at several anniversary screenings of *Enter the Dragon*, where he has been questioned on working on the movie and here are his answers to those questions:

Gil Hubbs and Bruce Lee in discussion on the banquet set.

How did you get involved with the project?

It was the first film I shot. I was doing mostly commercials and documentaries. I got a call from Bob Clouse (director of *Enter the Dragon*) in the middle of the night. It was a bad connection so I only heard every third or fourth word - but I did hear him ask, 'Do you want to come to Hong Kong?' So I said, 'Yeah, why not?' I had never seen a Kung Fu movie. I had never seen a martial arts scene. The only martial artist I had ever met was an instructor in the Marine Corps. I had never heard of Bruce Lee but I knew of Hong Kong. Bob told me he was shooting anamorphic but I didn't even know what that was. I had my American Cinematheque manual on the plane and I had to look up anamorphic, which I found out meant its widescreen. But I was a confident fellow.

Was Enter the Dragon *referenced against any traditional martial arts film?*

I don't think we referenced existing martial arts films. I had never seen one. I had never seen a scene from a Kung Fu fight, and I had never seen a martial artist on film. And Bob had done an action film, *Darker Than Amber*, which Bruce saw and liked, and Bob was an extremely inventive, visual guy. And he also was tough. So if things weren't going along, he would find a way to move forward - and there were a lot of obstacles. But I don't think that Bruce was able to express his ideal, so we just started - started with Scene 1, started shooting, and Bob knew how to make a film, and to navigate around the obstacles in the way. And I think Bruce maybe wanted it to be more like the films they were making in Hong Kong, and I think Bob realised that for it to do well around the world, it needed to be different. It needed to have a broader story and people identify it visual to be different. So they worked very closely together; they did have many discussions and disagreements, and Bob handled them very well, and Bruce was very talented.

Were the production team and crew ambitious to make the movie?

The ambition was not that grand for the people that made

Bruce Lee, Robert Clouse, Dave Friedman, Gil Hubbs and Fred Weintraub

Gil Hubbs looks on as Bruce Lee shouts to someone off camera.

the film. The ambition was to live through it. To live through the day, and in that day, try to advance in making the movie. The grand ambition, I'm sure it was there in an office some place, but Warner Bros. really was not involved at all. The producer over there, and Bruce, wanted to fulfil Bruce's ambition that it was a major kung fu movie. But it didn't really translate to the production.

What was the equipment like you used to make the movie?

For the crew it was, like the equipment, taking a step back in time, the tools for lighting were very simple. In Hollywood you had a lot of tools to control light, and over there I think we had window screens, black paper, rope, and clothes pins.

How did you like working with Bruce?

He was a nice guy to be around. He was fun. He was a very hard worker. He was a very talented athlete; he could do things with his body that are indescribable. And he had a group around him of other stunt people that he had trained, and he gave them a lot of respect. He was joking around with them a lot, but they made the movie a lot better, because Bruce had a lot of vigour in his acting and his physical ability and in his presentation of his martial arts. But if you take another person into it and fight him, that person has to have a like amount of vigour in reacting to it. Because I don't know if you knew this, but Bruce didn't kill everybody in the movie. They all got up and walked around. and sometimes we did Take 2 and killed them again. But I'd say most of the people that reacted from a punch from Bruce were masters at it. And that ability, and that ability to time it was amazing. When I looked at the film, that reaction had to be within three frames, an eighth of a second, and if it was a quarter of a second, it was wrong. And you couldn't really tell that on the set but Bruce could. And if he said, 'This is a miss,' we did it again.

Was there a special type of movie magic on the set?

I think there was a mix of magic; he was a magician. He was a mix of athletic ability, and a mix of a gunfighter. When you see gunfighter movies, they look at each other, and then the guns in his hand and he's shot. Bruce was like that - he would look at you and pull you in, and like David Friedman, the film's still photographer said, his eyes would pull in the camera, and he would decide with his eyes that he was going to hit you or kill you or whatever. And you saw that and thought, 'I'm not going to let him do it,' and it would happen. It was over. And you were still thinking 'I'm not going to let him do it,' as you're flying back. So I think it was a mixture of very dramatic, very vigorous ability, and he was extremely confident of himself. There is no one in the world he would not be able to defeat.

Did anyone in 1973 know, while in production, how big the film was to become?

No. Nobody did. It was going to be a good film. As we got along the road, it became evident that it was going to be good film, but if you categorise a martial arts film like *The Big Boss*, we knew it was going to be better, but on a worldwide stage. But no one knew that it would be anything close to what it became. No one! Maybe Bruce, however the producers, Warner Brothers, Bob and me, no. But Bruce and Linda I think they had an idea it would be a massive hit.

Bruce Lee ponders as Gil Hubbs prepares to shoot the sampans scene.

Bruce Lee, Robert Clouse and Gil Hubbs on the tournament set.

Gil Hubbs and Andre Morgan on the tournament set.

How do you think the film became more than a simple martial arts film?

Enter The Dragon grew into much more than a simple martial arts film due to Lee and Wall's collaboration.

What made this film inspire other action movies?

It says a lot that even though *Enter The Dragon* wasn't inspired by other films, it wound up being an inspiration in its own right. A large part of that is due to the collection of martial artists in its cast, but also a result of filmmakers willing to think outside the box.

How did the idea for the mirrors scene come into the film and how was it filmed?

It was Bob Clouse's idea. We were at lunch at one place and we were in a boutique that had vertical mirrors like what you see on one wall, and we said, 'That would be great.' But Bob came up with the concept of how to shoot it, which was a very simple scene to do and easy to light because there weren't a lot of options, other than being in the mirrored room which was very disorienting.

Bob's idea was - so that we wouldn't be seen - to build a closet and put mirrors on the outside of it. We would put the camera in there with me and Bob and the assistant. We cut a couple holes. If we wanted the camera here, we would move the closet to get that angle and just stick the lens through the hole. That complicated the image a lot because we were shooting into a mirror and the mirror bounced all around. You actually got nauseous in the room; you had to actually physically touch someone, because you might be talking to the wall. Bruce walked into mirrors; we all walked into mirrors a bunch of times.

But it was pretty easy to shoot because you could only put lights up above and they bounced all over the mirrors. When you turned on a light, everything was lit. The way to put lights up high was very restricted. It wasn't like a stage in Warner Brothers. So you were limited by the physical space. If there was room to put a light, then that would be a good place for a light. It was very difficult to direct the action because of the complication of the images. If you wanted Bruce to move in camera to the left, he had to move to the right. Bruce would say 'No - Han is right there, why I don't hit him.' We would have to explain that the camera doesn't see him there.

LALO SCHIFRIN
THE MUSIC OF ENTER THE DRAGON

Thanks to the recent screening of *How Bruce Lee Changed the World*, which was shown on the *Bio* satellite channel, we were able to secure an interview with the famous composer and music conductor Lalo Schifrin, who is best known in martial arts circles as the man behind the music to Bruce Lee's iconic film *Enter the Dragon*.

Lalo Schifrin was born in Buenos Aires on 21st June 1932. The son of a musician (his father was the conductor of the Buenos Aires Philharmonic), Schifrin studied music and composition before leaving for Paris in the 1950s. There he discovered jazz and became friends with famous musicians such as Michael Legrand and Stephane Grappelli.

Back in Argentina in 1956, he met Dizzy Gillespie and then joined forces with him in the United States where Schifrin immediately became successful as his arranger. The film producers were very interested in his unusual sound which was a mix of jazz, Afro-Cuban tradition and classic composition elements. In 1964 he scored the outstanding music for *Joy House (Les Felins)* by Rene Clement. Its main theme *The Cat*, became a hit.

From 1965 onwards, Schifrin regularly worked for the film and TV industry. He composed stunning soundtracks including *Cool Hand Luke* (1967) which was nominated for an Oscar, *Bullitt* (1968), and *Dirty Harry* (1971). He also worked on themes for TV series that have become real worldwide standards: *Mission: Impossible* and *Mannix* to name but two. Schifrin is still busy and regularly writes for the film industry; one of his recent efforts being *Rush Hour*, featuring Jackie Chan.

His film themes have become benchmarks and he is revered by today's DJs who love to sample his compositions, proving that Lalo Schifrin still inspires musicians throughout the world.

ENTER THE DRAGON

How did you get to do the Enter the Dragon *Music Score?*

I have to tell you the story. My older son liked to see martial arts movies. Nobody in the family liked to take him because the movies made in Hong Kong were sometimes terrible. Anyway, one day I said that I would go, and all of a sudden I heard my theme to *Mission: Impossible* in the score of one of these films. It was really the theme, not even a paraphrase and it was not a sample: it was a steal. There was also music from Quincy Jones' *Ironside*. I left the theatre a little bit mad. There was a Chinese composer who wrote most of the music for these films who was more or less trying to copy Morricone. But he was not equipped to do it. I said to myself 'I wish I could get to make the music for a movie like this one, because I could show them'.

I got home and the same day my agent called me to let me know that Bruce Lee, the biggest Asian star, was doing his first American film with Warner and that the producer wanted me to do the score. It's a true story. I have to be careful what I dream of wanting to do, because when I do, it happens. So I said 'OK'. I went to see the movie and there was quite a lot of music to write. I was given six weeks to write the score.

The producer called me in the middle of the third week. Bruce Lee was in town and wanted to meet me. I live in the west side of Los Angeles. In those days, with the traffic, it would take meat least one hour to drive there and one to drive back and the lunch another hour and a half. That meant if I went for that meeting I was going to lose three or four hours of work. I didn't know what I would say to Bruce Lee as I thought that we had very little in common. I said to the producer that my recording date was very close and that I had to deliver the score. I couldn't lose four hours for a lunch. The producer insisted, telling me that Bruce Lee was dying to meet me. 'Me?' I answered.

So I went and I met Bruce Lee in the Warner Bros restaurant. His whole body was like iron. Then he started to talk and he said, 'You know I studied five thousand years of martial arts tradition. Martial arts come from India and started with Indian monks who developed empty hand self-defence to protect themselves against bandits. Then their art went to China, Korea and Japan. It's a very old tradition.' Then he added, 'I learned the traditions in order to break the rules.'

THE 50TH ANNIVERSARY COMPANION

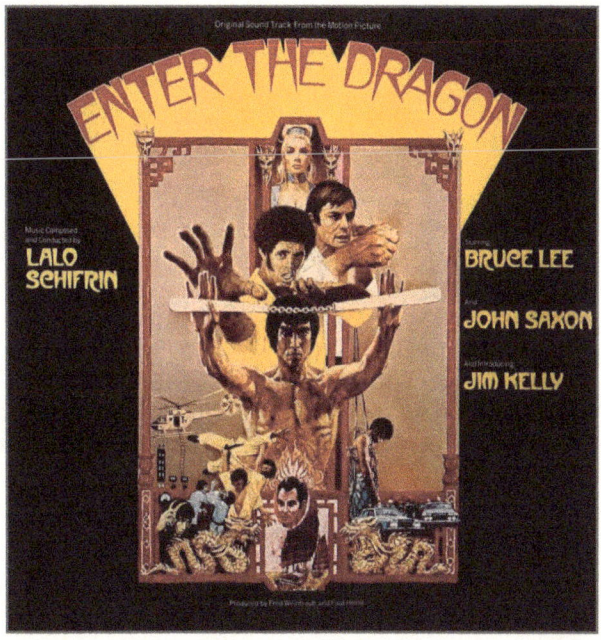

International Warner Bros release vinyl record for Enter the Dragon.

Japanese TAM release vinyl record for Enter the Dragon.

ENTER THE DRAGON

I replied 'Wahouh, I learned two thousand years of European music tradition in order to break the rules.' I realised that we had one thing in common. And then he said, 'The reason I wanted to meet you is because I practice everyday in my dojo in Hong Kong to the rhythm of the music from Mission: Impossible.'

Talking about the score; I found challenging not only the idea of doing what that Chinese was trying, unsuccessfully, to do, but also the idea of using Chinese music. I studied it very carefully. The idea was to combine oriental music with contemporary sounds. Wah-wah guitar was very prevalent. The score is a mixture of everything. It's a chemical combustion instead of being a physical mixture. It was really something more. That to me was challenging and I did it. The score became very popular especially among filmmakers today. When I was on the jury of the Cannes Film Festival in 1994, Quentin Tarantino won with *Pulp Fiction* and he said to me, '*Enter the Dragon* is my favourite score.' Brett Rattner, who directed *Rush Hour*, has the *Enter the Dragon* music on his answering machine! This is crazy.

Was the main theme released as a single?

Yes, but only in Asia, Japan and the UK. I got a gold record for that music.

How did you come to the idea of using Bruce Lee's shouts in the main title?

I did the first sampling, then when we went back to Pierre Henry again, we realized that anything was possible, the montage of sounds and music for instance. I found Bruce Lee's voice so interesting that I said to the producer of there cord, who was Larry Marx, that I wanted to include the voice of Bruce Lee. I asked him for a sample of the soundtrack and I knew exactly where to put it. It began with a strong introduction with this ostinato of guitars. It's almost like a response.

Did Bruce Lee like the idea?

Well, he was never able to enjoy the success of the movie because he died soon after the end of the shooting. People have lots of ways to explain his death. Some think that he was murdered. After I did that score, I decided that I would study Kung Fu and I started training, eventually becoming a black belt.

Every action dictates the style of music. How did the type of action in Enter the Dragon *dictate the style of the score?*

Well, first there was the idea of oriental music with contemporary American sounds. That was appealing. Then the use of slow motion I used synthesizers. I combined sounds using Chinese and Japanese folk instruments. I recorded the score in four sessions as there is a lot of music in the movie, it never stops. I couldn't record with ethnic musicians because I would still be in the recording room now. I mean they don't always know how to read music. What I did was to write Chinese music, trying to avoid the clichés. I cheated a bit using instruments that were not particularly Chinese, but when you write for oboes or something that is very vibrato, it does sound a little Chinese. I had cimbalom, the Hungarian instrument, played by a classical musician. But all this combined gave the feeling of an Oriental sound.

Was it a large orchestra?

Oh yeah, four French horns, lots of brass and percussions, One of the percussionists was Emile Richards who collects instruments from all over the world and he invents instruments from things you can buy in any stores, kitchen tools, house keys, anything. He makes wind chimes with keys that sound completely different. Actually, he said that for the score of *Enter the Dragon*, he used his whole house. He used to have all the instruments in a warehouse in his home. He plays them and he also rents them out to the studio. For this film he said that I played his house. I made a catalogue of instruments according to the scenes and used them for those scenes. There was a tablas, an India instrument which its equivalent in Cuban music would be bongos. It's not the same sound, but it's the same size. The congas are bigger, deeper. There is another Indian instrument, a sort of low table that I also used in the film. Stix Hooper from The Crusaders played the drums.

Enter the Dragon composer Lalo Schifrin at his piano.

Promotional soundtrack poster for *Enter the Dragon*.

DAVE FRIEDMAN
STILLS PHOTOGRAPHER

Dave Friedman first met Bruce Lee when they both worked on *The Green Hornet* TV series in the summer of 1966, where Lee was an unknown actor playing Kato alongside Van Williams titular character The Green Hornet. Dave was the First Assistant Cameraman assigned to the camera crew and he had no idea of Bruce's legendary skills when we began the show. Although the show was short-lived, it made Bruce a household name. While working on *The Green Hornet*, Bruce and Dave became friends and after he went back to Hong Kong, they stayed in touch and visited him several times during his many trips there. Bruce asked Dave to come and work on his films there but he was always too busy with his work in Hollywood to do that.

In late 1972, Mort Lichter, head of the Warner Bros Still Department, contacted Dave about working on their upcoming film *Enter the Dragon* that was to be shot in Hong Kong. Mort knew that Dave had spent a lot of time in Hong Kong and he also knew that Dave had known and had worked with Bruce. It took him about three seconds to say yes to the job.

When he arrived in Hong Kong in early 1973, he learnt that he was one of a very small group of American crewmembers that would be working on the film which included the Director Robert Clouse, Director of Photography Gil Hubbs, Producer Fred Weintraub, and Associate Producer Andre Morgan, the latter being an American living in Hong Kong and working for Raymond Chow. They were the ones who were on the set every day.

Dave thought that the film itself was an absolute joy to work on and Bruce was a real professional to work with. Bruce knew everyone's lines, knew what everyone was supposed to do and choreographed all of the fight scenes. Bruce was the real deal and could do more than what he showed in the film.

ENTER THE DRAGON

He had the best control of his body of anyone that Dave had ever known. Bruce once told him that he could kill a person ten different ways before he hit the ground and Dave was as sure as hell believed him.

Dave and Bruce enjoyed many special moments on that film but what he most remembers are the wonderful lunches that the American crew had with Bruce at the beautiful, old Repulse Bay Hotel. Sitting on their veranda and enjoying a wonderful buffet lunch while overlooking the South China Sea is something he would never forget. Bruce and Dave had several dinners together in Hong Kong but Bruce didn't like to go out very much because people who didn't believe that he could actually do what he did in the movies would often challenge him. Bruce never accepted these challenges but one time, when challenged on the set by a very stupid extra, he did accept and the fight was over with one fast kick to the idiot's teeth.

Dave recalled filming of the big fight scene on the grass

Linda Lee and Dave Friedman relaxing on the set of *Enter the Dragon*.

tennis court did have one very anxious moment when Bruce's hand was badly cut by the glass bottle held by Bob Wall who played the villainous Oharra. Seems the Chinese film industry at that time had never heard of the artificial candy glass bottles used regularly for such things in American films and they used a real glass bottle instead. Bruce needed to go to the hospital for stitches but being the professional that he was, he returned to the set later in the day.

Dave also remembered an unknown extra named Jackie Chan and even though he did not speak English at that time, he was a delightful man to work with.

When Dave finished this film, he went to Europe to cover the Motorcycle Grand Prix circuit. While he was at Monza in Italy for the Italian Grand Prix in July 1973, a fellow photographer, who knew that he was a good friend of Bruce's approached him and told him that he had heard that Bruce had died. He was in complete shock since he knew that Bruce was his age and in great shape. Needless to say, later in the day this was confirmed to him and he was deeply saddened. Bruce had asked him to work on his next film but obviously that would never happen.

When he attended a private showing of the film at Warner Bros, there was a great sadness, knowing that Bruce would never see the completed film or attend the premiere of the film.

ENTER THE DRAGON
A CULTURAL EVENT

Bruce Lee's popularity was already on the rise in this country, especially among the Chinatown communities, when *Enter the Dragon* premiered in the USA in August 1973. *Fist of Fury* had opened in the West End of London in July 1973, the day before he died; it broke all box office records at the Rialto cinema for normal performances, for first day, for first week and for two weeks run. During its first week at the Rialto cinema, *Fist of Fury* took £8,892, a record that would be broken the following year with the release of *The Way of the Dragon*, which took £11,167. In the time between those films, two very British happened - the Kung Fu Craze and censorship.

A few months prior to the release of *The Way of the Dragon*, *Enter the Dragon* hit British cinema screens in January 1974 and the Bruce Lee/Kung Fu Craze REALLY took off in this country. Indeed, *Enter the Dragon* became an international success and Bruce Lee became a worldwide phenomenon.

Enter the Dragon was submitted to the British Board of Film Censors (BBFC) for classification in August 1973, where Stephen Murphy was the BBFC Secretary at the time. On 23rd October 1973, with five cuts to the film, *Enter the Dragon* was classified as an 'X' certificate. In December 1979, James Ferman, who had taken over the role of BBFC Secretary, re-assessed the film, resulting in the nunchaku footage being removed (and so was the image of Bruce Lee holding the weapon on the cinema poster). Bruce Lee's many fans who was infuriated at the cuts, wrote to the BBFC, informing them of their displeasure at their mistreatment of a master at the height of his genius. A letter received back containing a detailed response from them dated April 1980, included the BBFC stating, "It is extremely unlikely that these cuts will be restored." The fans continued to protest.

In 2001, all previous cuts, including the nunchaku footage, were restored when the film was classified '18' for video.

What was the reaction to Enter the Dragon in 1973/74? Over the years, has the film critics' opinion of Enter the Dragon changed?

This is what film critics said about Bruce Lee and Enter the Dragon in 1974, shortly after the UK release:

> "Enter the Dragon….What a rotten old film it is. Rotten in all the ways you'd expect a Hollywood-backed Hong Kong based Karate sonatra to be; and old not only because its script is early, rudimentary James Bond, but also in the eerier sense that its star Bruce Lee, being some months dead, the whole exercise seems to belong to an already musty past, like all those posthumous Jim Reeves records. The appeal the film makes to necrophiliacs may well be perversely heightened by the fact that young Bruce Lee was so patently fit during his lifetime. His abdominal wall actually appears to be made of bricks, and the whipcord in his neck stands out like muscles. He can fell an opponent with a shriek and a swipe of whichever oaken limb he fancies extending and he frequently extends them so fast you cannot tell which one he has selected. Sometimes the shriek alone is enough. Lee can probably waggle his mighty ears as well, though these are hidden under his Cliff Richard haircut.
> His facial musculature does get in the way when it comes to speaking lines, but he has no trouble with his first two; "Hallo, Mr. Braithwaite" and "Have some tea," which he enunciates with such vicious clarity that you fear for Braithwaite's safety, not to mention that of the teapot, table and nearby flagstones and trees.
> Once we hit the island, all is ritual thuggery and choreographed pain, whether at the hand-to-hand or foot-and-mouth fighting tournament, or down in the subterranean opium plant. A little sex is allowed between John Saxon, a worn glamour-boy heavy with nylon hair, and the puffy starletette Ahna Capri and the token black, Jim Kelly, regales the villain Han with the disastrously accurate line, "Man, you come right out of a comic book."
> The only unique attraction is Lee in motion and more particularly the peculiar expression that invades his face during the fractional pause after he has crippled an opponent. It has all the surface signs of shocked disbelief, yet it carries with it a preening quality and a threat. Very primeval. A

couple of Han's lines, by the way, have a familiar Nuremberg ring: "We forge our bodies in the fire of our will", and "It is strength that makes all other values possible". Mr. Lee successfully rubs out the propagator of these thoughts; yet looking at his own austerely prancing demeanour, we cannot be at all sure that he doesn't subscribe to them himself."

Russell Davies
The Sunday Times, January 1974

"A good guy says to the bad guy; 'Man, you come right out of a comic book.' Believe me, man; ALL of the characters in Enter the Dragon *come out of a comic book – where the dialogue never rises above Zap! And Pow...The thin storyline serves as an excuse for battle scenes choreographed in the form of bloodstained ballet. Why Bruce Lee ever bothers to run away from his attackers beats me. He is as elusive as indestructible and as incredible as Batman is. When outnumbered, he sends opponents flying through the air with the flick of the wrist...you quickly forget the story and concentrate on the splendidly staged acrobatic fights...A pity the film has an X certificate because the final fight to the death scene between Han and Lee in a mirror-maze room is rousing schoolboy adventure stuff."*

Arthur Thirkell
Daily Mirror, Friday January 11th 1974

"If the current craze for Kung Fu and all things Oriental can be attributed to any one man, then that man must surely be Bruce Lee. Enter the Dragon, *the Eastern cult film in which he stars, has been playing to capacity audiences in the past few weeks....Death (and some swift and shrewd spade work by a platoon of publicists) had transformed a minor superstar into an international cult figure...'The brightest thing since Valentino and James Dean' the publicity man shouted. In private, however, they wondered just how far the Lee cult could be pushed – and for how long. Their anxieties were not without some foundation. Dead cult figures are notorious for their commercial brevity. Also, Bruce Lee was Chinese. And any film man will tell you that the West has*

Bruce Lee choreographing Peter Archer and Jim Kelly for their fight scene in the movie.

Bruce Lee jokes around with Yang Sze and the extras while rehearsing for *Enter the Dragon*.

always displayed a curious resistance to the idea of any long-term admiration of Oriental heroes.
To complicate matters, Lee, unlike Valentino and Dean, was not a good actor...on the other hand; Lee had many good and fashionable things going for him. He was an extremely handsome man. He looked like every schoolboy's idea of a storybook Chinese hero - that is to say, half-Western, half-Eastern. He was also enormously athletic, moving about in his films as if he had never heard of a pace slower than a flat-out sprint. Then, he was lucky that his films arrived at the time they did...Finally, he had good old-fashioned film star sex appeal....Even those who initially scorned to mention him, except in amused or contemptuous tones, are now changing their minds."

Merrill Ferguson
New Reveille, February 8th 1974

"Robert Clouse seems to have lost grip of the movie at various times and then tried to get back into the swing of things, but at that he doesn't succeed terribly well. The flashbacks, although meant in good faith, just do not have the solidifying effect that they should have, and the scenes where Lee is recruited into Mr. Braithwaite's secret organisation are terribly weak. The film itself doesn't seem to really warm up until the men are safely on the island and performing at the tournament....Not a really spectacular film by any means and it didn't really do justice to Bruce Lee's abilities. The film leant much too heavily on the spectacle of the Martial Art Tournament and did not make enough effort to create a really solid story out of the material given. This was not due to the director, Robert Clouse, alone, but to the terrible script supplied by Michael Allin. All in all, not a very satisfying experience."

Ian Findlay
Exciting Cinema Magazine, 1974

Throughout the years, *Enter the Dragon* has continued to receive similar reviews, such as Kim Newman's review in 2003, thirty years after the film's initial release that appeared in the book *1001 Movies You Must See Before You Die*. Kim Newman wrote: "Director Robert Clouse has the style you'd expect of someone directing a Brock Landers adventure (lots of zooms and flares) and Lee, whose real-life Hong Kong English was heavily-accented but fluent and distinctive, is stuck with Charlie Chan dialogue consisting of enigmatically wise pronouncements. But the action still delivers non-stop astonishment as, without the aid of the wires or effects used in the likes of *Crouching Tiger, Hidden Dragon*, Lee goes magnificently through the motions, twirling his signature nunchucks, flexing has oiled torso, influential on an entire genre of subsequent martial art movies and a template for every beat 'em-up computer game. *Enter the Dragon* wins its place in film history purely on the strength of Lee's charismatic presence and literally inimitable fighting moves."

The real importance of *Enter the Dragon* was realised after being the subject of much academic study. As it states on Wikipedia: "The film's themes generated scholarly debate about how they reflect the changes taking place within post-colonial Asian societies following the end of World War II".

In 2004, *Enter the Dragon* was selected for preservation in the United States National Film Registry by the Library of Congress as being "culturally, historically, or aesthetically significant."

In 2010, author Paul Bowman used cultural theory to analyse and assess Bruce Lee and used Bruce Lee to analyse and assess cultural theory in his book "Theorizing Bruce Lee". This included taking an in-depth look at *Enter the Dragon*. An example of his analysis is shown in the following excerpt: "One is clearly reiterated throughout Lee's oeuvre: it takes the form of the reiteration of the movement from superlative physical violence to supreme calm. In particular, one can clearly see it enacted and re-enacted regularly throughout *Enter the Dragon* (1973). Repeatedly, Bruce Lee fights, wins, stops, is utterly calm. He bests hordes of opponents, and then sits down in the lotus position. He kills a man, waits, and walks away. Amidst the mayhem of a mass battle, he sees his enemy, stops, ignores all else, walks towards him... The basic argument will be that this reiterated rhythmic cycle from stillness to explosive movement back to stillness encapsulates the fundamentals of the event and the communication of Bruce Lee. Accordingly, my proposal is that Bruce Lee was indeed a cultural event, and not merely a moment in the realms of cinema. Rather, this rhythmic motif, reiterated by Bruce Lee, actually enabled (or completed) a profound transformation both in Western discourses of the body and in Western bodies. It signals a displacement, a transformation, in many registers and realms: public, private, discursive, psychological and corporeal..."

Paul Bowman concludes in *Theorizing Bruce Lee*, ".....to locate Bruce Lee firmly at the shifting centre of enduring intercultural and cross-ethnic representation: A process in which the acceleration and intensification of contacts brought by technology and commerce entail an acceleration and intensification of stereotypes, stereotypes that, rather than simply being false or incorrect (and thus dismissible), have the potential of effecting changes in entire intellectual climates...(Chow 2002:63)."

Bruce Lee (and *Enter the Dragon*) will continue to be theorised and debated for many more years to come.

Bruce Lee aims a side kick to cameraman Gil Hubbs as John Saxon looks on.

Jim Kelly watches Bruce Lee as he throws a punch towards the camera.

WHEN BRUCE MET JACKIE
AND WHAT HAPPENED NEXT!

Although Bruce Lee was already established as an up and coming talent after his work in *The Big Boss*, its tremendous success afforded him to have much control over his next film with Raymond Chow's Golden Harvest Films. *Fist of Fury* stands alone as the catalyst to Bruce's phenomenal success.

This success came about because Bruce knew that with this film, he had to improve the quality of everything that went into film making in Hong Kong in the early 1970s. He had the good idea if he could bring some of the techniques he had learnt when he had been involved in filming TV and Hollywood movies in America and add the qualities of martial arts action that was specific to Hong Kong films - especially with his genius to make martial arts look amazing on the big screen - he could be on his way to becoming the top Chinese actor in Hong Kong and then maybe the world.

To achieve this, Mr Lee fought tooth and nail with Lo Wei, the director of *The Big Boss* and *Fist of Fury*, to make these changes, as Bruce knew that without them the film would definitely not have impact he wanted to explode on the screen and blow the Chinese audience away.

Lo Wei was a very competent filmmaker and had obtained both scripts for *The Big Boss* and *Fist of Fury* from a famous Hong Kong script writer Ni Kuang, but everything was a bit stale and set in their ways which often led to Lee having on set blazing rows, including the films official fight choreographer Han Ying Chieh who also came from the old school of film making. It is well documented and there is plenty of photographic evidence that Bruce took charge and responsibility for directing the action scenes and those that he participated in, you can notice there is a clear distinction between his directing style and that of Ying Chieh and Lo Wei. These scenes were, of course, most of the fights that Bruce had in the film, especially

ENTER THE DRAGON

the end fight scenes.

Apart from the fight scenes, a lot of other things were improved on *Fist of Fury*, including production, set design, costumes and music, which were all head and shoulders above other films at the time; it also had twice the budget of *The Big Boss*. Golden Harvest films went all out to recreate sumptuous indoor and outdoor sets to depict the look of 1930s Shanghai, plus Joseph Kuo's exceptional music score complimented the film by managing to bring to mind Lee's emotional state through the music.

Each of the fight scenes were worked out by Bruce and in each one, he wanted the audience to feel tired with the amount of energy on the screen; whether he was fighting fifty Karate students in a dojo with nunchakus or killing his teachers murderers, every fight had to have the 'wow factor' and none more so than the very end of the fight sequences in which Bruce delivers the killing blow to Mr Suzuki. This had to be a especially memorable with high impact; the idea was for a stuntman to be pulled back on a wire backwards through a Japanese paper wall and into the garden in response to Lee's death kick.

The top stuntman at that time was a young person called Jackie Chan who had been working on the film as an extra and doing a few stunts if required. In his own words from the Bruce Lee documentary *Martial Arts Master*, Jackie recalls how he first met Bruce Lee.

"Bruce Lee was working on *Fist of Fury* and there was not enough stuntmen, and also at that time I was the best stunt man in Hong Kong and Bruce needed a stunt man to double for the Japanese guy Mr Suzuki and go though the window, so they called me up and asked me if I could do that. I said, 'Yes, I can hide my body so it looks like the Japanese guy.' After I do the stunt, Bruce Lee came to help me because the stunt was quite difficult and he asked me my name. I said, 'It is Jackie,' and he said, 'Hey Jackie, you're good, you're great.' I learnt when Bruce Lee kick, don't move your eyes. If you move your eyes, you will not see Bruce Lee kick you. He was so fast; he was as fast as a human being could be. The only thing I have seen that fast is in a cartoon and as for speed, Muhammad Ali or Mike Tyson were not as fast as Bruce Lee. He was so fast, you still could not see him move."

This was Chan's first meeting with Bruce Lee and his contribution as a stunt double for Mr Suzuki and flying through the air has entertained and enthralled movie goers all over the world.

This was Jackie Chan's initial station meeting with Lee but it wasn't his only meeting, Jackie always remembers. "I was walking on the street near the Peninsular Hotel in Tsim Sar Tchoi and Bruce saw me. He said, 'Hi Jackie, where you going?' I replied, 'Hi Bruce, I am going to play bowling.' He said, 'A bowling alley? Can I go with you? I said, 'What? Yes of course but I am going to the bus station.' but when I turned around, he had ordered a taxi and taxis at that time were very expensive for me. As soon as we got to the destination, Bruce was this huge hero and everybody was saying, 'Look, its Bruce Lee,' so I started saying, 'Go away, no signing, no photos. I was like his bodyguard.' When we got to the bowling alley, he just sat there with his bell-bottom jeans; I always remember these and his platform shoes. He then just sat and watched me all day. I was playing bowls and I was very good, I think I played one and a half games, then suddenly I showed him how good I was. Then he said, 'Jackie, I think I am leaving,' so I sent him to the street. I got him a taxi and then something strange happened; he opened the door and turned around. I said, 'Goodbye Dragon Brother,' and then he turned around and tried to say something but nothing came out of his mouth, so he turned around and got in the taxi. The last thing I saw was his bell-bottom jeans and his platform shoes."

For all the memories Jackie Chan has, his best memory of working in the Hong Kong film industry is working with Bruce on *Enter the Dragon*. Again he had been working on the film as a stuntman and recalled, " I was behind the camera waiting and waiting and I could just see Bruce going mad hitting stuntmen with two sticks. I just ran up towards him going, 'Whaaa,' and suddenly my eyes went black because he had landed one stick on the side of my head. I felt a little dizzy and I looked at Bruce Lee as I fell to the floor. Bruce continued with the action and kept in character until the director said, 'Cut,' then he threw the two sticks down to the ground and said, 'Oh my God,' and ran to me and lifted me up. He said, 'I'm sorry, I'm sorry,' but actually I was not in pain any because I was young guy and I was very tough, but suddenly, I don't know why, I pretended it was very painful. I just wanted Bruce Lee to hold me as long as could, and then for the rest of the day, every time he looked at me, he asked me if I was OK. I think that was my best moment with Bruce; he asked me what style of Kung Fu I practiced and I said, 'Shaolin Style.' He said, 'OK,' and then he said my name over and over again."

Working with Bruce on *Enter the Dragon* may have been the last time Jackie saw Bruce Lee alive but it was not the end of his connection with Bruce Lee and the *Fist of Fury* story.

In 1976, Jackie became involved in the first sequel to *Fist of Fury* and it was also the first film in which Jackie Chan got top billing in *New Fist of Fury*.

Jackie Chan had been out of the film industry prior to getting the part. The popularity for Kung Fu movies declined after the sudden death of Bruce Lee, leaving Jackie an unemployed stuntman and film extra. So he moved to be with his family in Australia and once there became a manual labourer on a construction site by day and worked in a Chinese restaurant by night.

Some time later, he was contacted by Willie Chan (who became his manager) and asked if he would like to work on a movie a called *New Fist of Fury* with the newly formed Lo Wei Film company in Taiwan. Jackie jumped at this chance and went to Taiwan along with Lo Wei the original director of *Fist of Fury*.

Jackie was quite knowledgeable of the storyline as he had worked on the first one by the time he got the end of the film Jackie had taken the mantle from Bruce Lee and become the *New Fist of Fury* on the big screen, but Jackie was not happy with this as Lo Wei had intentionally made Jackie do moves to make him look like Bruce Lee and though it did not hurt his career, he never copied Bruce Lee's moves again. He did several more movies for Lo Wei under contract until he could get from his clutches before making his first Kung Fu comedy *Snake in the Eagles Shadow*.

So although Jackie did not appear in *New Fist of Fury* as much as a starring role should offer, it was a serious movie and held true to the original by employing many of the original cast to resurrect their roles. By watching both films, it easy to compare and observe the on-screen presence Bruce Lee had without taking anything away from Jackie Chan, who had his own persona.

THE 50TH ANNIVERSARY COMPANION

Now, more than forty years on, *Fist of Fury* entertains audiences of all ages and how fitting that this passionate and patriotic Chinese story has initially launched the careers of two of the greatest martial arts movie stars of all time in Bruce Lee and Jackie Chan.

Over the years, we have seen Jet Li and Donnie Yen also have success with this Chinese storyline, showing just how powerful it is, but how good would it have been without Bruce Lee leading the way and because of this, he will always be the one who guides others down this story path.

Bruce Lee grabs hold of Jackie Chan in the underground caverns on Han's island.

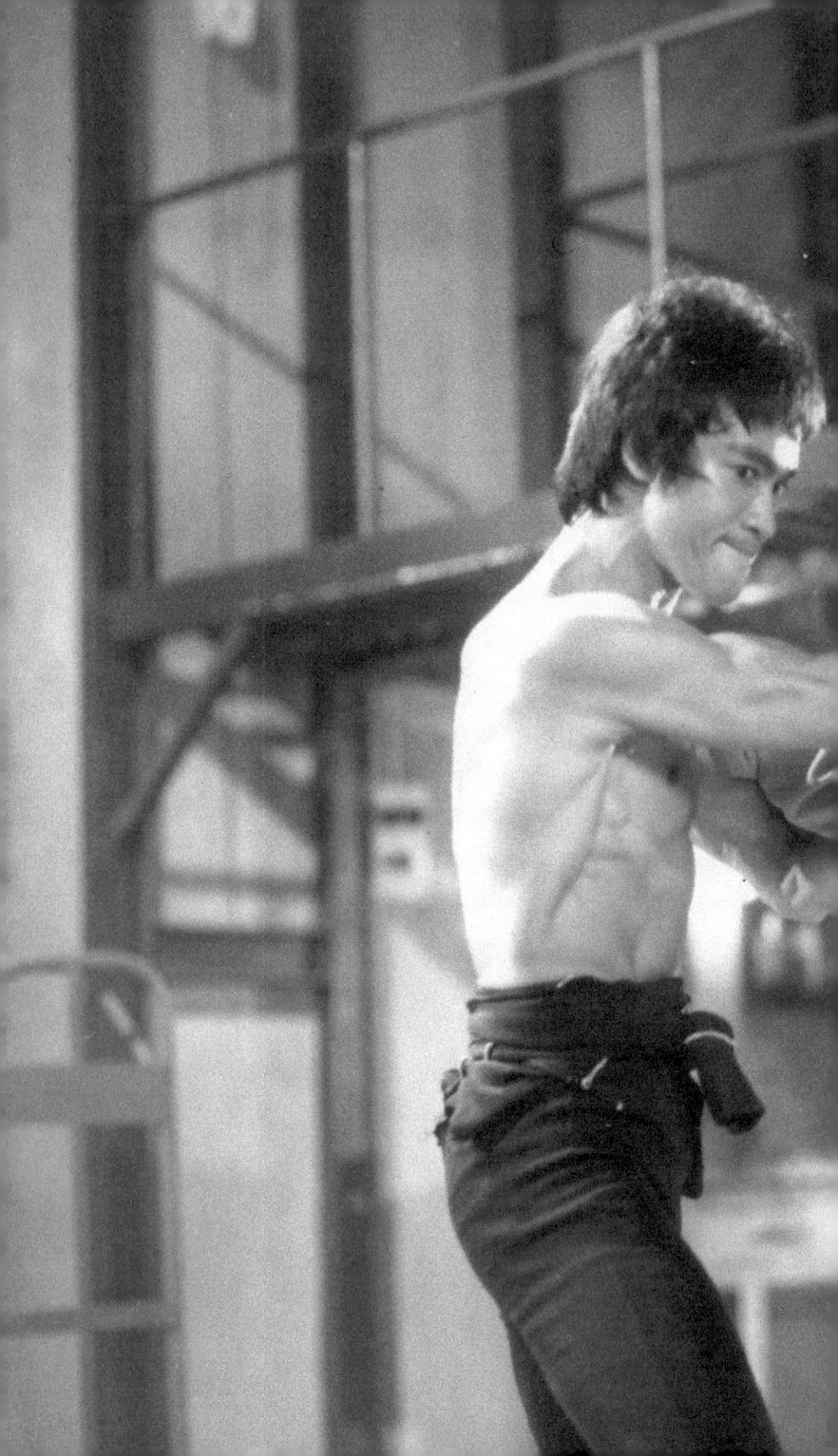

A wincing Jackie Chan prepared to get his neck broken by Bruce Lee. This was Chan's second movie with Lee; the first being *Fist of Fury*.

ENTER THE DRAGON
THE SAVAGERY OF BRITISH CENSORS

As *Enter the Dragon* celebrates its 50th Anniversary, it is hard to believe for some of the young people of today, that this iconic martial arts action movie icon was one of the most censored movies in the history of the British Board of Film Censors (BBFC). After its initial release, it was savaged by a couple of board members, who, to this day, feel just in what they did to this classic movie and all the others in Lee's portfolio. To celebrate the 50th anniversary of *Enter the Dragon*, here is the low down on how the film was cut, by whom, and why. It also delves into the murky underworld of bootlegs, created due to the demand by fans, to watch uncut Bruce Lee movies and how their passion for their hero became stronger and more intense than anywhere else in the world. There is something to be said about these cuts, as without them, the martial arts loving public may not have been so vitreous about their loyalty to Bruce Lee and the volume of popular demand was so great, that eventually the martial arts masterpieces were restored to their full glory as the censors faded into the sunset. British Bruce Lee fans got what they wanted 25 years after the films' initial releases. So as a tribute to the British Bruce Lee fans, here are the facts around the savage cuts to *Enter the Dragon*.

The film was Bruce Lee's final completed film and was submitted to the BBFC for classification in August 1973, one month after his death. Stephen Murphy, the then BBFC Secretary, felt that the film, like others in the wave of Kung Fu movies in vogue at the time, exploited violence purely for the sake of entertainment. He therefore considered such a presentation of violence without any qualifying context to be potentially harmful to teenage boys, to whom the BBFC recognised such films would be very attractive. While the highly choreographed fighting was viewed as a fantasy, the level of aggression, sadism and violence in the film could only be accommodated at the adult level. Hence the X category, restricting the audience to those aged 18 years and over.

Even if classified at X, Stephen Murphy deemed that *Enter the Dragon* would still require edits. These would remove visuals of a number of violent combat techniques that the Board considered excessive, and could be easily imitated by audiences. There was also concern about the violence being potentially encouraged by such a charismatic actor, at the height of his (posthumous) fame and popularity.

On 14th August 1973, an extensive cuts list was drawn up. Cuts were required to almost every reel and covered every aspect of the violent action in the film. However, in the end, only five separate edits were confirmed. In one or two cases, these were requests for reductions to the action rather than an outright deletion of the scene. These cuts included crotch kicks and neck breaks during fight scenes, and a sequence in which glass bottles are smashed and wielded as weapons. With these cuts made, *Enter the Dragon* was classified X on 23rd October 1973.

Nevertheless, the decision attracted criticism from both sides. Some members of the public felt the film was still too violent, voicing fears that it was dangerous and could encourage people to try Kung Fu for criminal purposes. For example, a cinema exhibitor from Bridgend secured a meeting with Murphy in January 1974 to discuss his concerns that a scene in the film, in which two police officers are beaten up and their

Yang Sze on the tournament set of *Enter the Dragon*.

Bruce Lee poses with his famous weapon, the nunchaku, in the caverns of *Enter the Dragon*.

> **BRITISH BOARD of FILM CENSORS**
> 3 Soho Square, London W1V 5DE
> President: THE RT. HON. THE LORD HARLECH K.C.M.G.
>
> Secretary: James Ferman   KRP/CRM
>
> Telephone: 01-437 2677/8
> Telegrams: CENSOFILM, PHONE, LONDON   22nd April 1980
>
> P Jagger
>
> Birmingham B38
>
> Dear Mr Jagger,
>
>   Over the years the Board has received many letters from kung-fu enthusiasts over our alleged butchering of the Bruce Lee films. Claims are made that such and such a scene has been reduced or removed and that we have destroyed visual examples of martial-arts fighting at its finest.
>
>   Board policy is quite clear. The only cuts that have been made in the Bruce Lee films are in those fights where nunchakas or chainsticks are used or where excessive kicks or punches to the head or crotch are seen. I would hasten to add that we are not worried that genuine students of kung fu will use chainsticks, but they are only a small part of the community. A far larger audience is continually being created as youngsters reach the age when they can see 'X'-rated films and we have evidence that the weapons they see in these films can be easily copied and used.
>
>   It must be understood that the Board has the full support of both the local authorities and the police in pursuing this policy and it is extremely unlikely that these cuts will be restored.
>
>   Many complaints are made, however, about variations in individual prints of films. This must be due to older prints being shown which have lost frames and sequences because of wear and have had to be re-joined by cinema projectionists. The Board has not made further cuts in any of these films except to remove some chainstick sequences in two of the early Bruce Lee films which were not cut at the time. No Bruce Lee film has been cut by more than five minutes and some far less than this.
>
>   Yours sincerely,
>
> K R Penry
> Assistant Secretary
>
> The Incorporated Association of Kinematograph Manufacturers Limited
> Registered number 117289 England
> Registered Office: 3 Soho Square London W1V 5DE

Letter sent to Peter Jagger from the British Board of Film Censors in 1980 regarding the censorship of Bruce Lee's films in the UK.

car stolen, could promote attacks on UK policemen. He urged the BBFC to remove the incident from *Enter the Dragon* and followed up his meeting with a series of letters. In a terse reply, Stephen Murphy responded to the one of the exhibitor's letters, "I can find no evidence that would support the point you are making."

Fans, particularly young ones, of both the genre and Bruce Lee, angrily protested the film's X certificate and the cuts imposed by the BBFC. One fourteen-year-old, who had recently taken up Kung Fu, wrote directly to the Board asking for permission to see *Enter the Dragon* in his local cinema.

This polite teenager was not alone; following the film's release in 1974, there are letters on file from members of the public reporting seeing children as young as 12 in screenings of the film.

The success of *Enter the Dragon*, and the Kung Fu genre in general, saw public concerns arise at the concurrent spread of the use of nunchaku (or chain sticks) and other martial arts weaponry among London youths. Media coverage of the issue caught the eye of James Ferman, Murphy's successor as BBFC Secretary. In December 1979, Ferman recalled *Enter the Dragon* for another look in the light of these anxieties. Ferman asked the film's distributor to remove sight of nunchakus in the fight sequence between Bruce Lee and his attackers. The images of nunchaku were also requested to be removed from the film's trailer and its promotional posters.

The removal of nunchaku, as well as other martial arts weaponry such as throwing stars and flails, soon became standard BBFC practice with the advent of VHS and Betamax bringing violent Kung Fu films into homes in the early 1980s.

When *Enter the Dragon* was classified for VHS in 1988, a kinder view of the film's violence was taken. The original five cuts were reduced to two, though sight of the nunchaku remained cut.

Throughout the 1990s, specific public concerns about nunchaku declined, while fears about more accessible weapons, such as knives, grew. Despite a modification to the BBFC's blanket ban of martial arts weaponry in 1991, when *Enter the Dragon* was re-submitted for video classification in 1993 and in 1996, cuts to sight of nunchaku in action were maintained.

In order for its policies to remain relevant and in tune with public feeling, the BBFC regularly reviews and adjusts them accordingly when issuing a new set of Guidelines. In 1999, the previous firm distinction between martial arts and other weapons was abandoned in favour of a more context-based, proportionate approach. Nevertheless, depictions of offensive weapons continue to be liable to cuts if they are considered likely to encourage violent behaviour in the real world.

Enter the Dragon was re-submitted and classified as 18 for home video in 2001, with all previous cuts (both to violence and weapons) fully restored.

ENTER THE DRAGON
AN IN-DEPTH LOOK AT BRITISH CENSORSHIP

Upon submission on 23rd October 1973 for *Enter the Dragon*'s theatrical release, the British Board of Film Censors (BBFC) requested several scenes to be cut but the exact length of cuts is unknown as only the censor's notes are available.

The censor's notes dictated the cuts to be made were as follows:

- The day after Lee goes out for his first night time investigation, Han demands his guards are punished. The BBFC demanded the scenes where Bolo breaks one guard's neck and another guard's spine to be removed plus the scene where their bloodied bodies are dragged away.
- In the Lee vs. Oharra fight, the BBFC demanded cuts to remove footage showing Lee kicking Oharra in the groin, O'Hara with the broken bottles and Lee stamping Oharra to death.
- The fight with Han and Williams to be trimmed to removed excessive violence.
- In the underground sequence, the BBFC demanded the removal of the scene where Lee snaps the guard's (Jackie Chan's) neck.
- During Roper's final battle with Bolo, the BBFC demanded the removal of the scene where Roper kicks Bolo in the groin and leaves him to fall.

In 1975, Stephen Murphy resigned from his position as BBFC Secretary and was replaced by James Ferman, who in 1979, requested that *Enter the Dragon* Be re-submitted for cuts to be made in addition to the ones already made in 1973.

The cuts requested in 1979 were to remove all sight on the nunchaku, not from just the film, but also from the trailers and promotional posters. It is entire plausible that the nunchaku poster ban initially only applied to cinema posters as the weapon was still clearly visible on the cover of the first few home

Bolo's fight with the guards in *Enter the Dragon*, which was partially cut by the British censors.

video cassette releases.

It would appear that the ban was only applied to the home video covers from 1988, with the formation of the Video Packaging Review Committee (VPRC).

When released on Home Video in the early 1980s, *Enter the Dragon* was released in four different version, yet only one was fully uncut and it was actually longer than the original theatrical release, as you'll discover. All four versions featured the same artwork on the front cover (apart from the second rental release stating 'Rental' on the front cover and spine) of Bruce Lee holding his nunchakus aloft but varied slightly on the rear cover and cassette labels.

The first version, released in December 1980 (VHS and Betamax) was intended for rental use only. It was the only fully uncut version released in the UK on video until 2001, containing footage that wasn't even in the original theatrical release from January 1974. In the very early days of home video, distributors were not required to submit their releases for classification, hence why it was released with the footage that the BBFC demanded be cut from the original cinema release. This release was not certified anywhere and featured a full synopsis on the rear cover with cast details being listed on a separate black card inside the case. The cassette tape for this version featured a white front and bottom label. The running time for this release was 94 minutes 51 seconds, though as stated in the Bruce Lee Society news sheets, the rear cover and cassette incorrectly states a running time of 86 minutes. Warner Catalogue No. PEVN1006

The next rental only version, released in 1982 (VHS and Betamax) was certified 'X' (rear cover and cassette label) and featured a condensed half-and-half synopsis and cast list on the rear cover. This version featured 'Rental' in red text in a blue box on the front cover and spine. The cassette tape for this version featured a blue front and bottom label. This was the first release of the movie to be released on home video after having a certificate from the BBFC. The cuts made, were the same ones requested in October 1973 to obtain a 'X' certificate for the theatrical release. The actual running time for this release was 94 minutes 30 seconds, equating to 21 seconds of cuts from the original home video version. The rear cover states a running time of 96 minutes. Warner Catalogue No. WEV1006

The first retail version, released a short time after its rental counterpart in 1982 (VHS and Betamax) was certified '18' (rear cover and cassette label). 1982 signalled a shift from the old 'X' certificate to the new '18' one. This release featured the same condensed half-and-half synopsis and cast list on the rear cover as the rental version. The cassette tape for this version featured a white and blue (old oval style) 'WB logo patterned' front and bottom label, which stated a running time of 96 minutes. The rear cover stated a running time of 95 minutes. However, the official running time for this release was again, like its 'X' certified rental counterpart, 94 minutes 30 seconds, having the same 21 seconds of cuts demanded for the theatrical and second rental releases. Warner Catalogue No. PEV1006

The second retail version, released in 1984 (VHS) was the last to use the original artwork on the front cover and the first one to be released after the Video Recordings Act (VRA) 1984 was brought in. It was certified '18' on the rear cover only, as the cassette carried no certificate. It featured the exact same rear cover as the first retail release (condensed half-and-half synopsis and cast list) and stated a running time of 95 minutes. The front cassette label featured the more modern 'shield-style' Warner Bros. logo used between 1984-1997, while omitting the bottom cassette label completely. The actual running time for this version was approximately 1 minute shorter than previous home video releases as the 1979 nunchaku related cuts would now have applied, due to the VRA. Also worth noting on this release was a hologram-type security sticker on the cassette. Early versions of the release featured the old oval logo on the security sticker, while later releases feature WHV. Warner Catalogue No. PEV1006 (Cover) No. 1006 (Cassette).

Warner Bros. re-submitted a pre-cut version film to the BBFC on 31st January 1988 for reclassification. The pre-cut submitted length was 94 minutes 27 seconds, which was almost the same cut version they released theatrically in 1974 and on home video in 1982. Not just content with these pre-made cuts, the BBFC demanded that the 1979 theatrical release cuts be replicated on video. The cuts made totalled a mammoth 1 minute 45 seconds and stated that every sight of the nunchaku should be removed from the film and the trailers. The Video Packaging Review Committee also came in force at this time, meaning that the video covers were also now subject

THE 50TH ANNIVERSARY COMPANION

The BBFC demanded a groin kick, broken bottles and Lee stamping O'Harra to death be cut from the movie, finally being restored several years later.

ENTER THE DRAGON

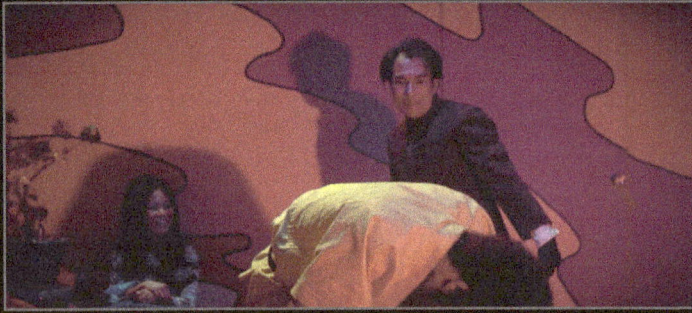
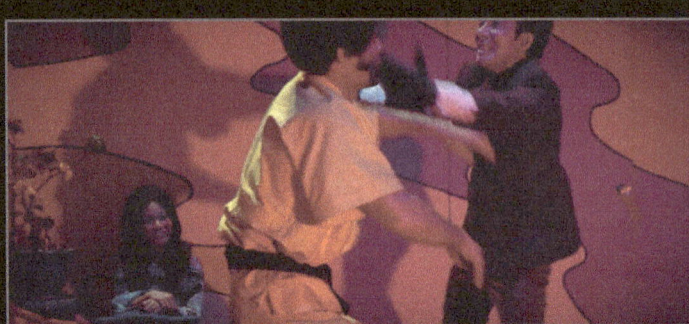

The British censors were not impressed by Han's destruction of Williams and therefore ordered several cuts, which were restored later on.

to the same rules that applied to the cinema posters and promotional material from 1979.

Two versions of this edition were released within a short time of each other from 1988, both having almost identical covers with the minor differences being on the rear cover and on the cassette itself. The front cover featured Bruce Lee in a fighting stance, covered in Han's inflicted scratches and standing in front of a green and yellow dragon. The rear cover was green in colour and stated that it was a "BBFC Edited Version." The cassette had a white label dotted the multiple instances of the modern shield-style logo and 'WARNER HOME VIDEO' at the top with *Enter the Dragon* printed underneath. This cassette label was the first to feature the BBFC's new (at the time) red '18' certificate.

This release stated the running time as 93 minutes on both the cover and cassette. The barcode number on the cover for this release was 5014780 100626, with the cassette displaying the number 1006.

The same version was re-released a short time later, identifiable by small variations on the rear cover and cassette. On the rear cover is a square under the images which states "Warner Home Video U.K. Limited". On the predominantly blue cassette label is new artwork with "*Enter the Dragon*" in the top left corner and the same red BBFC '18' certificate in the bottom right corner. This release kept the cover barcode number 5014780 100626 but the cassette displayed the BBFC No. VFA06743 in addition to the original number 1006.

In 1993, Warner Bros. re-submitted the film to the BBFC for the film's first Widescreen release. From the BBFC's records, it's clear that there was a little bit of optimism on the distributor's part as they submitted the film uncut at 94 minutes 57 seconds but again, the BBFC demanded cuts, this time totalling 21 seconds, but they did allow some previously cut scenes to be put back in such as Bolo breaking the guards' neck and spine, Lee stomping on O'Hara, Roper's Bolo groin kick, etc. and due to a change in policy, they had relaxed their position slightly on the nunchaku scenes. Instead of an outright ban, they could be seen on screen for a minimum amount of time in order to aid with the continuity of the film. The guards could be seen earlier in the film, holding nunchakus whilst patrolling the island, however, Lee couldn't be seen twirling them about but the guard could try to strike him with them, he could take them off him, the guard could react and Lee could strike one guard to fall into the water, before running off to become trapped, where he proceeds to sit down and hang them around his neck as Han tells him that, "the battle with the guards was extraordinary."

This release of the film had a running time of 94 minutes 33 seconds. The silver cover reverted back to the original poster artwork but had one obvious modification; Lee now held aloft a Bo Staff instead of his nunchaku as the BBFC hadn't changed their stance on that one. Also worth noting about this release, is the inclusion of an previously unseen, short 8-minute documentary, "A Legend in the Making."

The cover states a running time of 94 minutes for the feature and 102 minutes overall, with a barcode number 5014780 130630. The cassette featured new artwork with the orange WB logo in the centre, a running time of 94 minutes, a cassette number 13063 and a BBFC No. VFB 06096.

1996 saw the release of yet another release of the film. This time, Warner Bros. submitted a pre-cut version of 93 minutes 25 seconds to the BBFC, which, unusually, was 68 seconds shorter than the one they previously released. The BBFC passed this shorter version without any further cuts.

This Fullscreen edition had "SCREEN CLASSICS" at the top of the gold front cover and featured the same artwork at the 1993 Widescreen release, with the Bo Staff replacing the nunchaku. Also on the cassette was the same, "A Legend in the Making" documentary that was included with the 1993 release.

The cover stated a running time of 94 minutes for the feature and 102 minutes including the documentary, with a barcode number 5014780 010062. The cassette featured the same orange WB logo artwork, a running time of 94 minutes, a cassette number 01006 and a BBFC No. VFB 06194.

The final cut version was released in 1999 in Widescreen as the 25th Anniversary Special Edition on VHS but for the first time on DVD, was released as a non-Special Edition.

Submitted to the BBFC pre-cut on 13th November 1998, with a running time of 96 minutes 58 seconds, this version included previously unseen material featuring Lee speaking to the Shaolin Abbot just after his fight with Sammo Hung at the beginning of the film and him recalling that conversation during his 'Hall or Mirrors' fight with Han at the end but knowing

THE 50TH ANNIVERSARY COMPANION

Roper's kick to Bolo's groin wasn't so much the issue for the BBFC, but letting him fall afterwards was and so the scene was cut. A change in policy saw it restored later on.

the BBFC well by that stage, opted to take out the nunchaku sequence like the previous release, prior to submission. As well as the additional scenes, Warner Brothers made slight changes to the film's soundtrack including a mono to 5.1 conversion.

On a black background cover, a more modern twist on the original poster was used and the same one from the US release at the time with one alteration; Lee's Bo Staff remained. Included on the VHS as special features, were a Behind The Scenes Documentary, Original Theatrical Trailer, new documentary "Bruce Lee In His Own Words" and an all-new introduction by Linda Lee. The VHS cover stated a total running time of 131 minutes, 97 minutes for the feature and 34 minutes for the special features with a barcode number 5014780 159235. The cassette featured the same orange WB logo artwork as the previous release, the text "SPECIAL EDITION", a running time of 130 minutes, a cassette number 15923 and a BBFC No. VFC 07783.

As the DVD version wasn't the Special Edition, the cover didn't mention it and stated a running time of 95 minutes. The barcode number was 9321900 159210 with the number D015921 above it, while the disc displayed D1 15921.

For the first time since 1980, Enter the Dragon was released fully uncut in the United Kingdom on both VHS and DVD.

The BBFC Secretary James Ferman had retired the previous year and the board had begun to take a more context-based and proportionate approach to censorship but noted that depictions of offensive weapons would still be liable to cuts if they were likely to encourage violence in the real world.

Submitted on 31st July 2001, with a running time of 98 minutes 16 seconds, including the Shaolin Abbot and Hall of Mirrors scenes from the previously released 25th Anniversary Special Edition, the BBFC finally passed the film with no cuts for the first time ever. All previous cuts were reinstated and the British fans could finally, legally watch what the rest of the world had been able to see for the previous 28 years. Warner Brothers also kept the slight changes they made to the film's soundtrack for this release.

The VHS release marked the final time it would be available on that media and was presented in a thick cardboard case. Utilising the same cover as the previous release but with the nunchakus reinstated and bringing it in line with it's modern international counterparts, it proudly boasted of being the "UNCUT SPECIAL EDITION."

The VHS cover stated a total running time of 128 minutes, 98 minutes for the feature and 30 minutes for the special features with a barcode number 5014780 211216. The cassette featured the same orange WB logo artwork as the previous release, the text "UNCUT SPECIAL EDITION", a running time of 128 minutes, a cassette number 21121, a BBFC No. VFC 19454 and a holographic security sticker.

The DVD, having the ability to hold more video than previous formats allowed, contained even more special features than the VHS. Released in a cardboard and plastic "snapper" case with a dual-sided/single-layered disc, one side stored the film whilst the opposite side had the special features.

The cover stated a running time of 99 minutes with the barcode number 7321900 211215, with the number D021121 above. Printed around the disc's centre hole are the number 21121 and the BBFC No. VFC 26020.

Since 2001, several new DVD and more recently, Blu-ray versions have been released on home media in the United Kingdom, all of which have been the full uncut 25th Anniversary Special Edition featuring the additional Shaolin Abbot and Hall of Mirrors scenes plus the small soundtrack changes. These releases have included the dual-sided/single-layered disc being put out as a single-sided/dual-layered disc, a 2-disc edition, a red cover 2-disc edition, HD-DVD edition, several Blu-ray editions, a 40th Anniversary edition, plus several box sets. *Enter the Dragon* was also available as part of the *Hong Kong Legends Magazine & DVD Collection* by Deagostini.

It is interesting to note that the only uncut versions that were ever released in the United Kingdom with the original soundtrack and without the additional 25th Anniversary scenes, are the first ever 1980 VHS and Betamax editions.

In 2023, with their 50th Anniversary 4K UHD Blu-ray, Warner Bros. have finally released Enter the Dragon in its original uncut theatrical form, digitally remastered and looking better than ever. Its only taken them forty years to do it but we finally have Enter the Dragon, fully uncut and fully restored to its 1974 cinematic glory.

It has been extremely difficult to compile a 100% accurate list of cuts and reasons behind them for *Enter the Dragon*. This

Bruce Lee holds aloft his famous nunchaku. Cuts made by the British censors for over twenty five years resulted in a clunky edit to the film until being reinstated in 2001.

The BBFC weren't too impressed with Lee's breaking of Chan's neck and ordered audio cuts.

Bruce Lee's nunchaku; cut by the BBFC for over 25 years.

is because it was submitted several times; some submissions were recorded but some weren't. The 1973 submission is recorded but doesn't list the official passed running time and all we have is a case study on the BBFC website that states what cuts were ordered. The 1979 submission is not recorded at all on the BBFC website and is only mentioned in the same case study on the website.

The latest BBFC submission in July 2023 resulted in the certificate being lowered from 18 to 15 and the BBFC website lists content advice so that the millenials among us can avoid being too upset when watching an action movie. The latest content advice from the BBFC is:

violence
There are regular fight scenes, including with implied breaking of bones. People fight with blades and other weapons, drawing blood.

sex
A man picks sex workers from a line-up. There are allusions to group sex.

sexual violence and sexual threat
A gang of men pursues a woman, touching her inappropriately despite her clear discomfort. There are references to women being kidnapped and trafficked.

nudity
There is breast and buttock nudity in a sexualised context.
It is implied that a woman takes her own life.

There are references to the misuse of drugs, including opium. Sequences of moderate threat see characters put in danger by foes who seek them harm.
There is infrequent use of a racist term ('jig'), but discrimination is clearly condemned by the film as a whole.
Mild bad language is used ('bloody', 'bullshit'), as are milder terms ('damn', 'hell').

CUT HISTORY

As provided on the BBFC website as of 23/07/2020:

Date	Submitted	Passed	Cuts
23/10/73	Submitted Time 99m 9s	Passed Time N/A	Cuts N/A[1]
31/01/88	Submitted Time 94m27s	Passed Time 94m41s	Cuts 1m45s
10/11/93	Submitted Time 94m57s	Passed Time 94m33s	Cuts 21s
26/01/96	Submitted Time 93m25s	Passed Time 93m25s	Cuts None
13/11/98	Submitted Time 96m58s	Passed Time 96m58s	Cuts None
31/07/01	Submitted Time 98m16s	Passed Time 98m16s	Cuts None
17/07/23	Submitted Time 98m17s	Passed Time 98m17s	Cuts None

[1] Running time in film format. No cut details available on BBFC website but a Case Study on the website gives some notes.

ENTER THE DRAGON
THE MISSING PIECES OF A CINEMATIC JIGSAW

After the release of *Enter the Dragon*, Golden Harvest had to decide what to do with the footage for Bruce Lee's final uncompleted project, *The Game of Death*. After years of discussions, a new script was written by *Enter the Dragon* director Robert Clouse, under the pseudonym Jan Spears.

Released in 1978, *Game of Death* was less than favourably received by Lee's faithful following, who had eagerly waited half a decade to see their hero in action again. Their five years of wait brought them just ten minutes of Lee, much to their disappointment.

Two years after the release of *Game of Death*, and with pressure from the Japanese film industry to release a sequel, Raymond Chow signed off on *Game of Death II* (also called *Tower of Death* in some countries).

The King of Kung Fu no longer being around didn't stop Chow from featuring Lee in the sequel and so he headed back to the Golden Harvest vaults to see what footage was available to include in the movie.

The scenes used in *Game of Death II* were just generic quick interlinking shots here and there, apart from three particular scenes which didn't make it into the final cut of *Enter the Dragon*.

In the first scene, Lee enters his room on Han's island with a holdall and closes the door before walking over to a yellow gi he notices hanging on the wall. He grasps the gi and studies it for a while before aggressively letting go of it in disgust. He hears the chirping of a small bird behind him which is in a cage hanging from the ceiling. Turning around, he playfully whistles at the bird as he glimpses a book on the top of a writing desk in the corner of his room. He places his holdall on the bed and walks towards the table, where he picks up the book, studies the cover and turns it over. As he turns it over, there is a

ENTER THE DRAGON

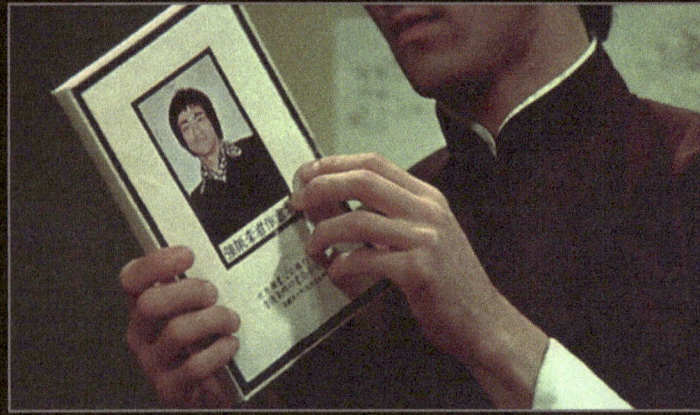

Bruce Lee inspects his room shortly after arriving on Han's island and sees a copy of his own book on the desk, having been placed there by Han.

photograph of Lee on the cover along with the Chinese text for "Shaolin Kung Fu." Lee smiles as he puts the book down and turns around to take in the rest of the room. This scene from *Enter the Dragon* is then followed by footage filmed specifically for *Game of Death II* as part of the story. The text on the book is roughly translated as, "Shaolin Temple Zhenqiang Martial Arts - Part Three," while the text under the photograph Lee on the reverse side states, "The Author of Zhenqiang Martial Arts."

In a script for *Enter the Dragon* dated 7th December 1972, it states the following:

```
MONTAGE - LEE
FOLLOWING Lee as he approaches the palace: noticing ter-
rain, cover, placement of guards, architecture of the
palace, mentally mapping what will be pockets of shadow
in the night.


INT. LEE'S ROOM
Lee enters. The room is furnished with a writing table
and a sleeping mat on the polished wood floor. Oriental
paintings grace the walls.


WRITING TABLE
Three books stand between a container of pens and a vase
holding a single lotus blossom, Lee smiles when he sees
the books... He takes one.


CLOSE SHOT - BOOK
The title is in Chinese. On the back, we see a photo-graph
of Lee, the author.


CUT TO:


INT. - WILLIAMS' ROOM
Williams' room is furnished with a large canopied bed, and
the walls are covered with posters.


CLOSE SHOT - POSTERS
CAMERA PANS over a vast panoply of Black — Angela Davis,
Eldridge Cleaver, Malcolm X, Muhammed Ali... and posters
showing the action in Black films.


CLOSE SHOT - WILLIAMS
He turns his head and sees, all alone on one wall, a poster
of a giant black fist. There is also a stereo tape-deck.
Williams turns it on, experimentally. He HEARS "The Horn."
He looks around, shaking his head in disbelief.
```

ENTER THE DRAGON

                    WILLIAMS
            All this... and Miles makes it cool.

INT. ROPER'S ROOM
Roper's room has a wide waterbed, and
Regal. Roper picks up the bottle and recites the label,
mumbling it to himself as in prayer, with his eyes closed.
A KNOCK interrupts him.

                    ROPER
            (with a wave of his hand, as if summing up
                his whole philosophy of life)

                    YES!
            All this and now Tania enters.

                    TANIA
            Welcome to our island, Mr. Roper.

                    ROPER
                (looking her over)
            I am very glad to be here.

                    TANIA
            Are your accommodations satisfactory?

                    ROPER
                (looking her over)
            They're wonderful, Miss... uh..,?

                    TANIA
            I am Tania.

                    ROPER
            Tania, That's Russian, isn't it?

                    TANIA
            I wouldn't know.

                    ROPER
    Yes, Tania, it's Russian. It means, "The Unexpected."

He lets it sink in.

                    ROPER
                (continuing)
            Will I see more of you?

                    TANIA
                (promising)
            Tonight... (pause) ... at the festivities.

Lee walks with the Abbot in a philosophical scene not included in the film until 1998.

From reading the script, it is evident that the scene from *Game of Death II* is from *Enter the Dragon* and takes place immediately after arriving on Han's island and just before the banquet. It is Han's way of letting his guests know that he has investigated them and knows them thoroughly; Lee has a copy of his book, Williams has posters of black icons adorn his walls with his favourite music on the cassette deck and Roper has a bottle of his favour Chivas Regal brand Whisky. Han had done his research on every single one of his guests and wanted them to know so, although he hadn't been as thorough as he should have been when it came his old fellow Shaolin disciple.

A second *Enter the Dragon* scene used in *Game of Death II* was an interaction between Roy Chiao's Shaolin Abbot and Lee, which takes place after Lee's opening battle with Sammo Hung. In the scene, the two men philosophically discuss Lee's thoughts when facing an opponent and the intricacies of Shaolin Commandment No.13 before moving on to discuss renegade Shaolin monk Han's treachery and the recently arrived Mr. Braithwaite. The audio in *Game of Death II* was dubbed into English and bore no resemblance to the actual dialogue that would have featured in *Enter the Dragon*. The original dialogue featuring Lee's own voice from this scene was featured on the vinyl record *My Way of Kung Fu* in 1977, thought is was not complete.

When Warner Brothers were putting together a 25th Anniversary Edition of *Enter the Dragon* in 1998, they restored this scene, however not with the original recorded dialogue. Due to it being incomplete, they asked the Bruce Lee Estate's chief historian John Little- who has also contributed his award-winning documentary *Bruce Lee: In His Own Words* to their new upcoming DVD release of the movie – to impersonate Lee's voice for the scene. Little was reluctant to record the dialogue but did so under the pretence that Warner Brothers would use it as a "scratch track" for engineers and professional voice artists to work with in order to create a new recording. However, Warner Brothers didn't create a new recording, nor did they use the original dialogue with Lee's voice. Instead they used Little's impersonation for the final version, much to the fans' and Little's own disappointment.

Also on the 25th Anniversary Edition of the film, they added a clip of Lee in the Hall of Mirrors where he remembers the Shaolin Abbot's advice of, "Destroy the image and you will break the enemy," from their conversation at the beginning of the film.

A scene from *Game of Death II* features a slightly extended conversation from *Enter the Dragon* between Lee and the Old Man where they discuss Lee's sister and her tragic demise. There are a few seconds of splices here and there that don't feature in *Enter the Dragon* but surfaced in *Game of Death II*.

The *Enter the Dragon* script dated 7th December 1972 contains the following dialogue:

```
LEE
Lee is writing at his desk in his library. Piles of books
and papers lie neatly around him, and to the side, an
electric typewriter. A teapot and cup stand on a corner
of the desk, Lee's appearance is markedly different: he
wears reading glasses, and casually elegant clothes.

PULL SHOT - LIBRARY
The door opens and the old man enters, crosses quickly
to the desk. The room's walls are lined with books from
ceiling to floor and the wood floor and desk shine with
the light of a fire.

OLD MAN
The old man stands and watches Lee. Lee continues to
write. The old man lifts the teapot, helft is briefly,
then pours tea into Lee's cup. The SOUND of tea filling
the cup is very loud in the silence.

LEE
Lee's eyes move from his writing to the slowly filling
cup, then up over his glasses to the face of the old man.
Lee leans back, smiling curious. The old man is quiet,
hesitant.

                    OLD MAN
                 How is it going?

                      LEE
                    Very well.

                    OLD MAN
             How near finishing are you?

                      LEE
Almost done. Will you read it before I send it off?
```

ENTER THE DRAGON

```
                    OLD MAN
                As always.

A pause. Lee studies the old man.

                    LEE
            Would you like to read it now?

                    OLD MAN
                Not now. When it is finished.

                    LEE
            Then it is something else that you want to speak of.

                    OLD MAN
                It Is a very difficult thing.

                    LEE
                I can tell.

                    OLD MAN
                When is Han's tournament?

                    LEE
                Ah, the difficult thing.

The old man nods.

                    OLD MAN
            Before you decide, I must tell you something.

                    LEE
                (gently)
                All right.
```

Lee chats with the Old Man about his new book before being told the story surrounding the death of his sister.

                            OLD MAN
        The last of Han's tournaments was held in Macao three
                years ago. I was there with your sister.

The first eight lines of dialogue from the above passage is present in the *Game of Death II* footage and the majority of the rest is altered slightly in the final version of *Enter the Dragon*. A slightly longer shot of Lee writing at the beginning on the conversation turned up on streaming websites a few years ago.

As part of the 25th Anniversary Edition, Australian documentary maker Walt Missingham contributed a twenty minute film for Warner Brothers to include. Unfortunately, the documentary was never used but surfaced online a few years later and revealed some interesting unseen "outtakes" between Lee and Betty Chung's character Mai Ling. Over the years, other poor quality "outtakes" have been swapped and shared on VHS, DVD and streaming websites. Even though Chung's character only appears briefly in the film, as indicated in the script, she originally had a much bigger part to play.

The clips involving the two, take part in Lee's room; in one set of clips, Lee is wearing a white Mandarin shirt which he later removes to change into the black catsuit and in the other clips, Lee is wearing a navy blue Mandarin jacket.

In the film, Lee and Mai Ling have their first discussion just after Tania parades the girls around the competitor's rooms. Immediately after the discussion, the film cuts to Lee warming up the next morning in his room when he notices Oharra staring at him by the door. After the first day of fights, Lee silently changes into his catsuit and exits via the window, while Mai Ling looks on.

After the second day of fights where Lee kills Oharra and Han later reveals Williams' hanging corpse to a bewildered Roper, Lee already in his catsuit, jumps down from an external his second night time exploration of the island, before finally being caught.

It was often thought that the Lee and Mai Ling footage was outtakes from their first encounter but the different clothing worn by Lee in the clips suggest otherwise.

The *Enter the Dragon* script from 1972 reveals that Lee and Mai Ling have two conversations. In that script, the fights at the

Robert Clouse directs Betty Chung ready for her to arrive at Lee's room for the first time.

tournament, Bolo killing the guards and Lee killing Oharra, all take place over one day, instead of the two days in the final version of the film. In that script, Lee has his first discussion with Mai Ling and he heads out to explore the island. The next day, Bolo kills the guards, Williams has his fight, Roper has his fight, Lee kills Oharra, Williams is killed by Han, Lee has his second discussion with Mai Ling and heads out into the night again, before being trapped in the caverns by Han.

The 1972 script states the following about Lee and Mai Ling's first encounter:

```
INT. LEE'S ROOM-CLOSE SHOT-MAI LING
stands in Lee's doorway.
```

                        MAI LING
I am honored, sir, that you have asked for me.
However, please understand, these are not my duties.

Lee closes the door.

                                LEE
                       (reassuring her)
                         Please stay.

                             MAI LING
                    There are other girls...

                                   LEE
I want to talk to you — (pause) — Mai Ling.

She is startled to hear her name.

                             MAI LING
                   Where do you come from?

                                   LEE
                            Braith...

Her fingers fly to Lee's lips, silencing his voice.

                                   LEE
                  (continuing; whispering)
                        Braithwaite.

Mai Ling points to the sleeping mat, and gestures silence. Lee sits down on the mat to wait as she goes around the room blowing out the candles.

SLEEPING MAT
Lee watches Mai Ling as the light dims around him. In darkness, she joins him.

> MAI LING
> (whispering close)
> Han is everywhere!

> LEE
> Have you seen anything?

> MAI LING
> Nothing conclusive. I am kept in the palace, watched always... perhaps even now. I know nothing of Han's activities away from the palace. But I can tell you this: people disappear.

> LEE
> Who?

> MAI LING
> The girls. Every one of them. They are summoned to Han in the night, and the next day they are gone. All go, eventually. Some sooner than others. I know my own time is...

She breaks off as her voice weakens.

> LEE
> We'll get you out of here. Where is the radio?

> MAI LING
> Radio? I know of no radio.

> LEE
> Braithwaite says there is a radio.

> MAI LING
> Not in the palace — hidden somewhere on the island, then.

> LEE
> And our evidence against Han is probably with it.

Lee gets up, takes something out of his bag. He slips into a black jumpsuit.

> MAI LING
> (the strain beginning to show)
> You must be very careful. This is an evil place: nothing is as it seems. Trust no one.

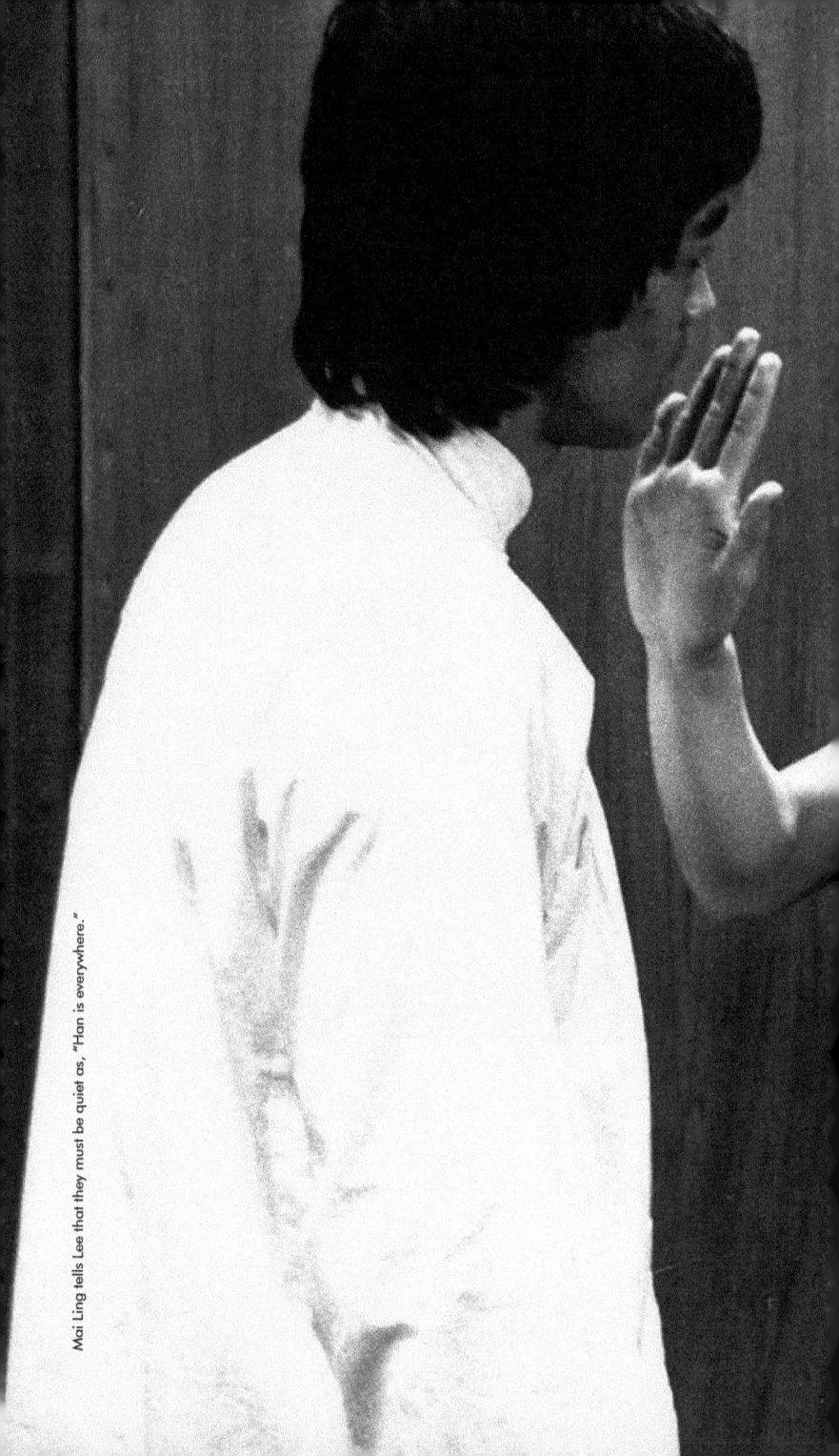

Mai Ling tells Lee that they must be quiet as, "Han is everywhere."

```
Lee goes to her, wipes silent tears from her face.

                    MAI LING
          I am glad they have sent you.


                    LEE
               Wait for me.

          He slips out the door.
```

The footage with Lee in the white shirt from the Walt Missingham documentary and the other footage from *Game of Death II* match this script extract perfectly when put in the correct order. It makes perfect sense when you put the dialogue with the footage and you can even lip read the word, "Braithwaite," as Lee says it. Every line of dialogue now has the footage to accompany it. From a context point of view, it works but from a narrative point of view, it works even better. We now have a more accurate reason why Lee heads down into the caverns; he's on the hunt for evidence against Han and to find a radio that Braithwaite has told him exists.

The other footage with Lee in a navy blue jacket takes place towards the end of the film, immediately after Roper is shown Williams' body by Han.

The 1972 script states:

```
          INT. BATH - LEE, MAI LING
     Lee and Mai Ling are meeting alone in the room.

                    LEE
     The radio has to be down there in the cavern.

                    MAI LING
          I will show you the elevator tonight.

                    LEE
          No. I'll go down from outside again.

                    MAI LING
               But why?

                    LEE
     The elevator is likely to be guarded, or have some kind
     of alarm. And if I should be caught, they'd know about
          you. When the tournament is over, you'd be...
```

Lee exits through the door on his first night time exploration of the island as he tells Mai Ling, "Wait for me."

ENTER THE DRAGON

> MAI LING
> No one leaves this island. You and the other men are prisoners now, also.
>
> LEE
> Roper and Williams will join us then.
>
> MAI LING
> No. Roper has joined with Han.
>
> LEE
> What!
>
> MAI LING
> And Williams has disappeared.

Lee is shocked silent. As Mai Ling waits for him to speak, they are startled by VOICES entering. They cannot leave. There is no place to hide. Without hesitation, Mai Ling unties her robe.

> MAI LING
> (continuing)
> Into the bath!

Bruce Lee and Betty Chung having a discussion in between filming.

BOLO, GIRLS
Bolo comes through the plants with three girls. They enter
the far end of the bath.

LEE & MAI LING
Lee and Mai Ling sit at the other end. Lee relaxes back
against the side of the bath as Mai Ling bathes him.

                    MAI LING
                  (continuing)
              Tonight is all we have.

Followed later by:

INT. LEE'S ROOM - LATE NIGHT - LEE, MAI LING
Lee and Mai Ling sit together on the sleeping mat. Lee
wears his black Jumpsuit. Mai Ling watches him tie knots
into a new length of his rope. He coils the rope and puts
it into his shoulder-bag. He stands up to go. Mai Ling
stands up. They look at each other Mai Ling nods. He
touches her face. He goes to the window, and out.

"But why?" asks a confused Mai Ling (Betty Chung) when told by Lee (Bruce Lee) that he will risk using the elevator on his second night-time visit to the underground caverns of Han's Island in a deleted scene from *Enter the Dragon*.

ENTER THE DRAGON

Bruce Lee shares a joke with Gil Hubs as he frames Betrry Chung off camera as he prepares to exit through the window on his second night time exploration of the island.

Like the first encounter between Lee and Mai Ling, the footage matches the script almost perfectly. There isn't a bath and Bolo doesn't enter with three girls but the majority is there. The words "Williams" and "Roper" are easily able to be lip read by looking at the footage of Lee speaking. The footage from the final version of the film where Lee packs his bag with rope and exits the window on his first journey outside the palace is clearly from his second journey near the end of the film, as explained in the script. The second encounter between Mai Ling and Lee according to the script, clarifies why Lee goes through the window the second time and not the door. It also explains the urgency to prowl the island to find the radio in order to get them out of there.

In conclusion, if the footage was included in the film, despite it containing no new fight scenes, it explains things in much more details and gives a motive for actions not fully explained. Like the recently rediscovered and re-released Mandarin Cut of *The Big Boss*, this footage breathes new light into a classic movie and greatly improves the narrative; something that the people at Warner Brothers are unable to see.

ENTER THE DRAGON
THE GLOBAL IMPACT OF AN ICON

Fifty years after its release, Bruce Lee's film *Enter the Dragon* has stood the test of time as one of the greatest martial arts movies ever made. What is equally impressive is the global impact that *Enter the Dragon* has had, not simply in the world of film, but also in the world of martial arts and the world of philosophy. In this article I'd like to take a look at the film's effect in each of these realms, and the effect the film had on me.

FILM

Before *Enter the Dragon*, the majority of martial art films that were being made in Hong Kong were mainly costume dramas full of swords and spears, blood and gore - usually in which a single man fights twenty or thirty armed opponents - what Bruce Lee referred to as "one long, armed hassle."

Enter the Dragon set the gold standard for martial arts movies. One of the first American-Chinese co-productions, while its production values may not have been high according to Hollywood standards, they were according to Hong Kong standards and the current standards of the genre at the time.

The film also introduced the world to Bruce Lee, who proceeded to show audiences, especially those in the West, something they'd never seen before; amazing martial art action. Lee revolutionized the way combat was presented on screen. His action choreography was far superior to anything else out there; his fight scenes were mesmerizing and unlike anything seen before in martial art films. Lee's fights were choreographed like deadly balletic dances, and watching Lee in action was like watching a world-renowned ballet dancer such as Nijinsky, Nureyev or Baryshnikov as they danced; the perfect confluence of grace, speed and power.

Enter the Dragon propelled the martial arts into the world-

Bruce Lee and John Saxon outside the Golden Harvest studios.

wide cinematic mainstream and popularized martial arts in a global scale, which caught the attention of Hollywood and made them sit up and take notice.

The success of *Enter the Dragon* fuelled the sales of kung Fu films worldwide; Lee's earlier Chinese films were dubbed in English and released in the US and elsewhere. Other Hong Kong martial art films started popping up at cinemas, often presented in poorly dubbed and crudely re-edited versions. However, as I said, *Enter the Dragon* raised the bar of the genre dramatically and the majority of martial arts films that followed over the next several years fell far short.

Enter the Dragon's global impact with regard the world of film and filmmaking cannot be denied or overstated. At Lee's time, there were no Asian stars that had achieved international acclaim as a leading actor in a Hollywood film. That was because the people in power at the studios did not believe that an Asian actor would be able to draw a major audience. Bruce Lee proved just how wrong they were. Lee's achievements as an actor, director, writer, producer, and action choreographer have inspired countless individuals of every ethnicity all over the world to pursue their dreams in the world of film and television. Filmmakers and actors across the globe cite Bruce Lee as their inspiration and guiding influence to want to make movies --

If *Enter the Dragon* had never been made, would America and the rest of the world have been introduced to and entertained by the likes of Jackie Chan and Jet Li? Would filmmakers such as John Woo and Ang Lee have broken through into mainstream Hollywood as directors? Would Chuck Norris have made it to the big screen and television? Would films such as *Bloodsport*, *The Karate Kid*, and *Teenage Mutant Ninja Turtles* have been made? Personally, I don't believe that anyone else could say for certain. But I do know that *Enter the Dragon* opened the floodgates.

MARTIAL ARTS

Enter the Dragon also had global impact on the world of martial arts. Audiences watching the film were blown away by the incredible fight scenes. Kids everywhere began imitating Lee, choreographing their own fight scenes, kicking and punching at each other, swinging nunchakus about in the air.

Bruce Lee demontrates to Tony Liu how he wants him to attach John Saxon during their fight scene.

Many people, intrigued by the beauty and deadly precision of Bruce Lee's martial artistry, decided to begin studying martial arts themselves. Some searched to try and find a place where they could find instruction in Lee's martial art of Jeet Kune Do. Others began training in Karate, Judo, Ju Jitsu, or Kung Fu.

Martial arts schools began popping up everywhere. Some were legitimate schools, others were not. Over the course of time, a number of phony JKD schools purporting to teach Lee's art and philosophy began appearing both across the United States and around the globe. Wing Chun Gung Fu, the martial art style Lee studied for four years as a teenager in Hong Kong, received a lion's share of the publicity, and today there are branches of Wing Chun being taught in martial art schools in all parts of the world. *Enter the Dragon* was also instrumental in the development and proliferation of the many hybrid martial arts that have come into existence over the years since the film opened. Inspired by Lee, many martial artists began training in different martial arts at the same time, combining stand-up striking methods with grappling and ground fighting systems, etc. People grabbed bits and pieces from this art and that art and mixed them together, and terms such as "non-classical," "self-expression," and "cross-training" became martial art buzzwords.

With regard to the world of mixed martial arts, Bruce Lee is widely recognised as a pioneering force and some people have even referred to him as "the godfather of mixed martial arts." A number of UFC and MMA fighters including champions such as Tito Ortiz and Anderson Silva have credited Lee as their inspiration for getting involved in martial arts.

PHILOSOPHY

While certain Asian philosophical concepts and ideas existed in some of the martial arts systems being taught at the time *Enter the Dragon* came out, they were not in any way a large part of the cultural mainstream in America or many other countries.

Enter the Dragon introduced and shared aspects of Asian philosophies such as Taoism and Zen with Western audiences (many of them young people) for the first time. Furthermore, the film did it in a way that was both fascinating and that peo-

ple could relate to.

This was not philosophy as taught in the school classroom or argued over by members of the philosophical academia, but "philosophy in action." Lee not only verbalised Zen concepts such as "Wu Hsin," or "no-mind" ("I do not hit, it hits all by itself") and Wu Wei (no striving), he embodied these principles in his physical actions. For example, in the cavern fight scene in which Lee fights a multitude of opponents while waiting for an elevator, Lee suddenly hears people coming up behind him, turning around, he lets his mind remain spontaneous and unattached and responds to the attacks spontaneously and effortlessly, his actions so automatic and reflexive that they seem divorced from conscious effort. Maintaining fluidity of thought and action, he is able to respond naturally to the situation and 'fit-in' with his opponents to defeat them.

Other philosophical concepts such as "the art of fighting without fighting" and the necessity for "emotional content" in one's actions were also given physical illustration throughout the film.

In the early 1970's many Americans were searching for different ways of thinking and different ways of approaching life in an attempt to replace rigid religious or belief systems that for one reason or another failed to fulfil their emotional or spiritual needs. *Enter the Dragon* offered these people a glimpse at a potential alternative which might be of benefit to them. As a result, people who otherwise would probably have not even been interested in the subject began investigating Asian philosophical frames of thinking such as Taoism and Zen. Many began drawing and absorbing various elements from these and other philosophies into their own personal belief systems and using them or adapting them to fit their own lives.

As a side-note, interest in Bruce Lee as a contemporary philosopher has steadily increased over the years, and books containing his philosophical thoughts and ideas have sold millions of copies.

MYSELF

It was Bruce Lee who ignited my passion for martial arts, watching him in action on *The Green Hornet* television show when I was a kid. When *Enter the Dragon* opened in thea-

Robert Clouse directs Bruce Lee in his room on the set of *Enter the Dragon*.

John Saxon and Bruce Lee take time out from filming *Enter the Dragon*.

tres, I had been training in JKD under Sifu Dan Inosanto in his backyard for almost two months. The memory of Lee's untimely passing was still fresh in my mind and I'd seen Dan devastated by the loss of his teacher and close friend. I had seen several small clips of the film which had played at the time of Lee's death, but they were only 1-2-minute excerpts. Nothing prepared me for what I saw when I attended the film on opening day at Mann's Chinese Theatre.

Sitting in the darkened cinema and witnessing Bruce Lee in action on the screen was an experience I shall never forget. Lee's speed, power, and cat-like movements, coupled with his sheer intensity was electrifying. I was also captivated by the philosophy that Bruce put forth throughout the film. The martial arts were not just about something physical; they were about philosophy in action.

And while I realised that Bruce's fighting actions in the film could be labelled as "cinematic JKD," watching *Enter the Dragon* made me more determined than ever to learn everything I could about his art and philosophy.

CONCLUSION

The world of film has changed a great deal from when *Enter the Dragon* hit the screens. There have been incredible technological advancements in the world of film-making with the use of such things as computer generated images, special effects, etc. It could be very easy for someone today to look at *Enter the Dragon* and say, "Oh, it's not that good, look at the movies we have today." And while that may be true in some aspects, speaking as someone who was there at the time it came out, I can say without reservation that *Enter the Dragon* eclipsed every other martial art that existed at that time and for years after.

In his book, *The Fist That Shook The World*, author Lou Gaul, wrote, "Lee displayed the majesty of martial arts to people everywhere and, to put it mildly, the world has never been the same." I think these words pretty much sum up the global impact that *Enter the Dragon* has had.

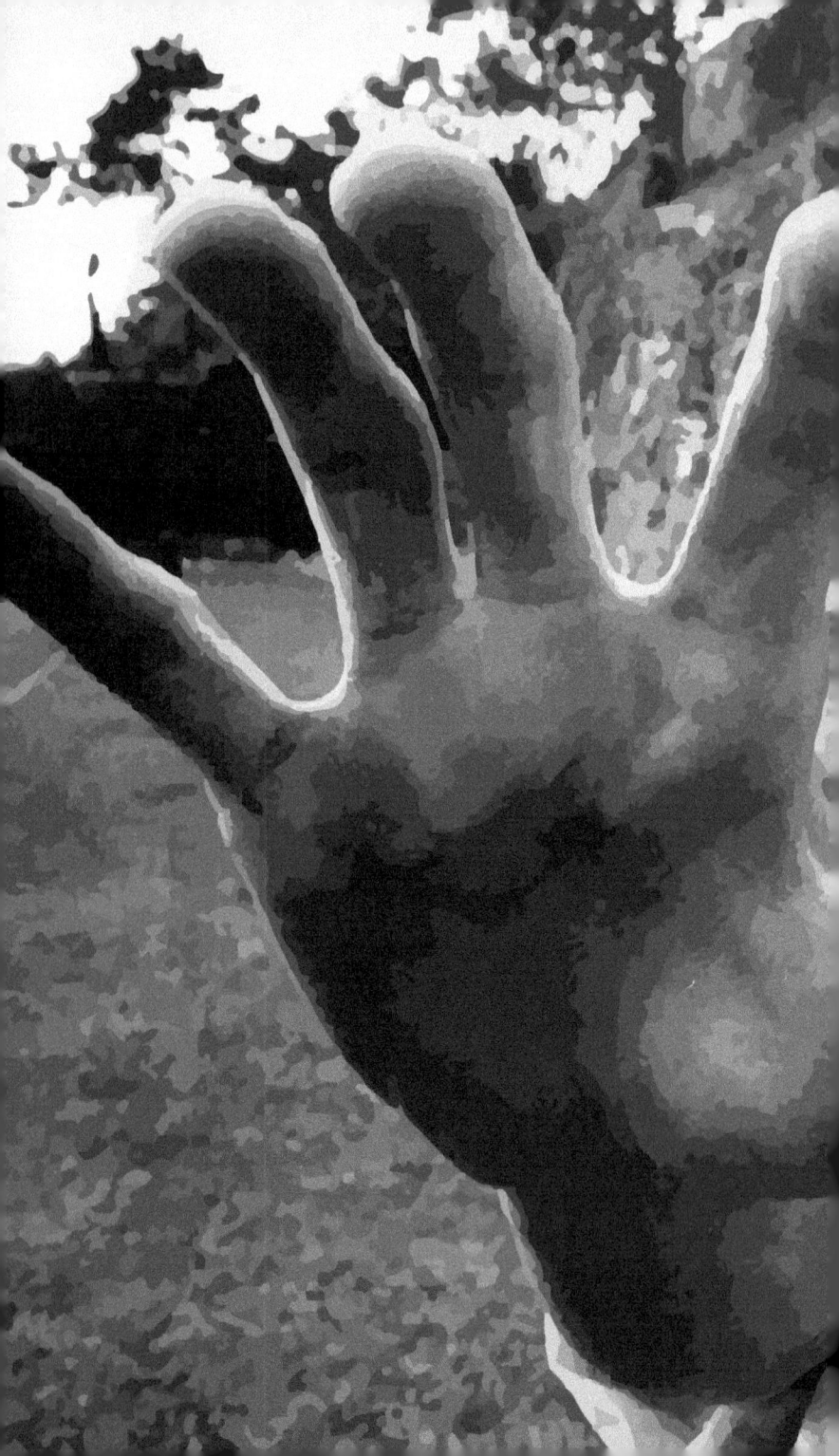

SELECTED FILMING LOCATIONS

OPENING FIGHT SCENE
HO SHEUNG HEUNG
SHEUNG SHUI, HONG KONG

MEETING WITH BRAITHWAITE
TSING SHAN MONASTERY
HONG KONG

BRAITHWAITE'S FILM REEL
HYATT HOTEL
HONG KONG

SAMPANS SCENE
ABERDEEN HARBOUR
HONG KONG

LEE'S CEMETERY VISIT
THE MUSLIM CEMETERY
HAPPY VALLEY, HONG KONG

HAN'S ISLAND
PALM VILLA TENNIS COURTS
(NOW THE AMERICAN CLUB)
TAI TAM, HONG KONG

HAN'S FORTRESS
KING YIN LEI
WAICHAN, HONG KONG

ROPER GOLF SCENE
GRIFFITH PARK GOLF CLUB
LOS ANGELES, USA

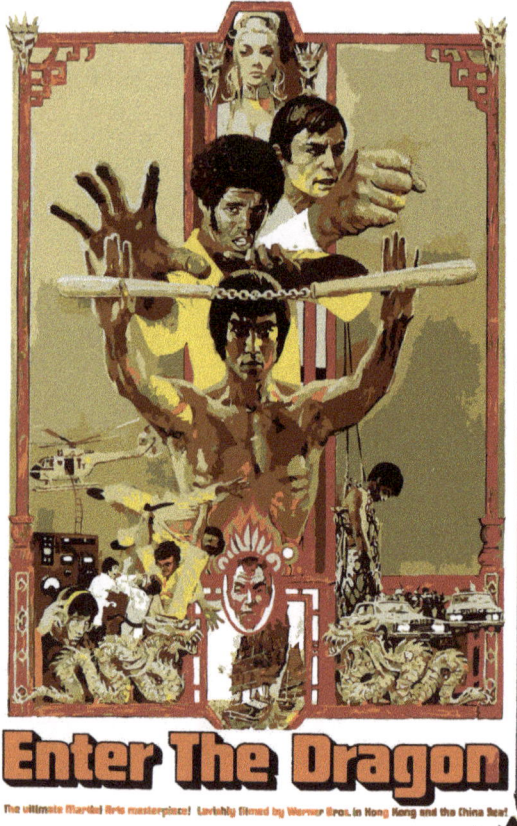

THE 50TH ANNIVERSARY COMPANION

CAST AND CREW

Production

Robert Clouse	Director
Raymond Chow	Producer
Paul Heller	Producer
Leonard Ho	Producer (U)
Bruce Lee	Producer (U)
Andre Morgan	Assc. Producer (U)
Fred Weintraub	Producer

Writing Credits

Michael Allin	Written by
Bruce Lee...	Written by (U)

Cast (Credits Order)

Bruce Lee	Lee
John Saxon	Roper
Jim Kelly	Williams
Ahna Capri	Tania
Shih Kien	Han
Robert Wall	Oharra
Angela Mao Ying	Su Lin
Betty Chung	Mei Ling
Geoffrey Weeks	Braithwaite
Yang Sze	Bolo
Peter Archer	Parsons
Ho Lee Yan	Old Man
Marlene Clark	Secretary
Allan Kent	Golfer
Bill Keller L.A. Cop	
Mickey Caruso	L.A. Cop
Pat Johnson	Hood
Darnell Garcia	Hood
Mike Bissell	Hood

Rest of Cast
(Listed Alphabetically)

Linda Lee Cadwell	Party Guest (U)
Billy Chan	Cave Guard (U)
Jackie Chan	Thug in Prison (U)
Lung Chan	Party Guest (U)
Shao-Hung Chan	Referee (U)
Ling Wei Chen ...	Guard (U)
Chok-Chow Cheung	Monk (U)
Roy Chiao	Shaolin Abbott (U)
Alan Chung San Chui	Guard (U)
Fat Chung	Han Traitor (U)
Robert Clouse	Thugs #1 (U)
Paul M. Heller	Radio Operator (U)
Hsing-Chun Hsu	Guard (U)
Sammo Kam-Bo Hung	Shaolin Fighter (U)
Chiu Jun	Guard (U)
Phillip Ko	Guard (U)
Yung-Sheng Kuo	Guard (U)
Jen Kwan	Party Guest (U)
Ching-Ying Lam	Fighter (U)
King-Chu Lee	Ohara's Crew (U)
Tony Liu	Fighter (U)
Keye Luke	Han (Voice) (U)
Hoi Mang	Ship's Mate (U)
Mars	Han Traitor (U)
Antone Pagán	Shaolin Monk (U)
Yao-Kun Pan	Ohara's Crew (U)
Yun-Sheng Pan	Ohara's Crew (U)
Steve Sanders	Instructor (U)
Chin-Lai Sung	Han's Guard (U)
Tai-Bo	Ohara's Crew (U)
Mi Tien	Mi Tien (U)
Wilson Tong	Ohara's Crew (U)
Wei Tung	Lao (U)
Yeung Wah	Guard (U)
Niki Wane	Williams' Girl (U)
Tian-Lin Wang	Party Guest (U)
Donnie Williams	nstructor (U)
Vincent Kwok Wing-Sing	Guard (U)
Chieh-Chiang Wu	Guard (U)
Ming-Tsai Wu	Han Traitor (U)
Tadashi Yamashita	16mm Footage (U)
Hua Yang	Guard (U)
Tau Wan Yue	Guard (U)
Biao Yuen	Fighter (U)
Bun Yuen Guard (U)	
Wah Yuen	Fighter (U)

Music

Lalo Schifrin	Music Composer

Crew

Gil Hubbs	Dir. Photography
Kurt Hirschler	Editor
George Watters	Editor
Peter Cheung	Editor (U)
Sheng-Hsi Chu	Art Direction
Sheng-Hsi Chu	Costume Design
Kuo-Hsiung Chen	Makeup Artist
Gary Morris	Makeup artist (U)
Wah Kam	Unit manager
Louis Sit	Prod. Manager
Chaplin Chang	Assistant Director
Yao-Chang Chih	Assistant Director
Lu-Po Tu	Assistant Director
Wen Tu	Assistant Director
Shun-Chang Huang	Props
Ping Wong	Sound

Stunts

Bruce Lee	Choreographer
Mickey Caruso	Stunts (U)
Jackie Chan	Stunts (U)
Sammo Kam-Bo Hung	Stunts (U)
Pat E. Johnson	Stunts (U)
Ching-Ying Lam	Ass. Action Dir (U)
	Stunt Double: Han
Mars	Stunts (U)
Charlie Picerni	Stunts (U)
Kien Shih	Stunts (U)

ENTER THE DRAGON

Robert Wall	Stunts (U)
Tau Wan Yue	Stunts (U)
Biao Yuen	Stunt Double (U)
Wah Yuen	Stunt Double (U

Camera & Electrical Department

Hsu Chen	Still photographer
Hui-Jan Cheng	Electrical Gaffer
Charles Lowe	Camera Operator
Dave Friedman	Still Photographer
Gary Graver	Second Unit
Henry Wong	Camera Operator

Music Department

Eugene Marks	Music Editor
John Audino	Trumpet (U)
Robert Bain	Guitar (U)
Israel Baker	Violin (U)
Max Bennett	Bass (U)
Hoyt Bohannon	Trombone (U)
Dennis Budimir	Guitar (U)
Larry Bunker	Percussion (U)
Larry Carlton	Guitar (U)
Vince De Rosa	French Horn (U)
James Decker	French Horn (U)
John Ellis	Reeds (U)
Clare Fischer	Keyboards (U)
Ralph Grierson	Keyboards (U)
Richard Hazard	Orchestrator (U)
Stix Hooperdrums	Percussion (U)
Ronny Lang	Reeds (U)
Bernie Kaai Lewis	Guitar (U)
Jack Marsh	Reeds (U)
Richard Nash	Trombone (U)
Antone Pagán	Percussion (U)
Richard Perissi	French Horn (U)
Joe Porcaro	Percussion (U)
Dorothy Remsen	Harp (U)
Emil Richards	Percussion (U)
Jerome Richardson	Reeds (U)
George Roberts	Trombone (U)
Joe Sample	Keyboards (U)
Lalo Schifrin	Conductor (U)
	Orchestrator (U)
Sheridon Stokes	Reeds (U)
Tommy Tedesco	Guitar (U)
Tony Terran	Trumpet (U)
Al Vescovo	Guitar (U)
Dan Wallin	Scoring Mixer (U)
Peter Woodford	Guitar (U)
Eugene E. Young	Trumpet (U)

Script & Continuity Department

Hua Ku	Script Supervisor

Additional Crew

Madalena Chan	Executive Assistant
Hua Kan	Prod. Assistant
Andre Morgan	Asst. to Prod (HK)
Jeff Schechtman	Asst. to Prod (USA)
Louis Sit	Asst. to Prod (HK)
James Wong	Sunset Supervisor
Bruce Lee	Teaser Writer (U)
	Voice Dubbing (U)

THE 50TH ANNIVERSARY COMPANION

WRITING CREDITS

ENTER THE DRAGON: A SYNOPSIS
BY CARL FOX AND ANDREW STATON

ENTER THE DRAGON: A HISTORY
BY ANDREW STATON

ENTER THE DRAGON: BROUGHT TO BOOK
BY ANDREW STATON

"YOU WANT TO BET?"
JOHN SAXON IS ROPER IN ENTER THE DRAGON
BY ANDREW STATON

AN INTERVIEW WITH
ENTER THE DRAGON'S JOHN SAXON
BY CARL FOX

THE UNSEEN ROPER
BY ANDREW STATON

SHIH KIEN: A TRIBUTE TO MR HAN
BY ANDREW STATON

JIM KELLY: HIS THOUGHTS ON BRUCE LEE,
ENTER THE DRAGON AND HIS FILM CAREER
BY ANDREW STATON

BOB WALL: THE MAN WHO WAS OHARRA
BY PETER JAGGER

BOLO YEUNG: THE CHINESE HERCULES
BY ANDREW STATON

**ANGELA MAO YING
THE FIRST LADY OF KUNG FU**
BY ANDREW STATON

SAMMO HUNG: THE DYNAMIC MAESTRO
BY ANDREW STATON

AHNA CAPRI & THE 8MM FILM FOOTAGE
BY ANDREW STATON

PETER ARCHER: FIGHTING WITHOUT FIGHTING
BY ANDREW STATON

GEOFFREY WEEKS: THE CHIEF OF MI6
BY ANDREW STATON

BETTY CHUNG: THE FEMALE SECRET AGENT
BY ANDREW STATON

ROY CHIAO: THE SHAOLIN ABBOTT
BY ANDREW STATON

TONY LIU: ROPER'S OPPONENT
BY ANDREW STATON

PAT JOHNSON: IT'S THE DOUGH ROPER!
BY ANDREW STATON

**YUEN WAH: THE MAN WHO MADE
A DRAGON LOOK AMAZING**
BY ANDREW STATON

ROBERT CLOUSE: DIRECTOR
BY ANDREW STATON

FRED WEINTRAUB: PRODUCER
BY ANDREW STATON

PAUL HELLER: PRODUCER
BY ANDREW STATON

**RAYMOND CHOW: THE MAN WHO
HELPED CREATE A DRAGON**
BY PETER JAGGER

ANDRE MORGAN: ASSOCIATE PRODUCER
BY ANDREW STATON

MICHAEL ALLIN: THE WRITER OF A CLASSIC
BY ANDREW STATON

GIL HIBBS: CINEMATOGRAPHER
BY ANDREW STATON

**LALO SCHIFRIN: THE MUSIC
OF ENTER THE DRAGON**
BY ANDREW STATON

DAVE FRIEDMAN: STILLS PHOTOGRAPHER
BY ANDREW STATON

**ENTER THE DRAGON
A CULTURAL EVENT**
BY PETER JAGGER

**WHEN BRUCE MET JACKIE AND
WHAT HAPPENED NEXT!**
BY ANDREW STATON

**ENTER THE DRAGON AND THE
SAVAGERY OF THE BRITISH CENSORS**
BY ANDREW STATON

**ENTER THE DRAGON: AN IN-DEPTH
LOOK AT BRITISH CENSORSHIP**
BY CARL FOX

**ENTER THE DRAGON: THE MISSING
PIECES OF A CINEMATIC JIGSAW**
BY CARL FOX

ENTER THE DRAGON
THE GLOBAL IMPACT OF AN ICON
BY CHRIS KENT

EDITOR AND DESIGNER
CARL FOX

CONTRIBUTING EDITOR
ANDREW STATON

COPY EDITING
CARL FOX

BOOK LAYOUT AND COVER DESIGN
BY CARL FOX

SPECIAL THANKS

JIM MCKEOWN, CHRIS THOMPSON, DAVE FRIEDMAN, KIERAN CLARKIN, JULIAN KEEN AND MINGXUE DU

ENTER THE DRAGON
ABOUT THE CONTRIBUTORS

CARL FOX was a staff member of the Bruce and Brandon Lee Association and a writer for *Impact*, *Martial Arts Illustrated* and *Eastern Heroes* magazines.

His first book, *The Bruce Lee Society: A Retrospective Look at Bruce Lee Mania and the Kung Fu Craze of the 1970s* was released through Promethean Press in April 2021.

His latest works, The *Kung-Fu Monthly* Archive Series, contains a modern authorised presentation of the complete library of the iconic Bunch Books publications. His work has been featured in several newspaper publications including The *Barnsley Chronicle* and *The South China Morning Post*.

Carl is a Karate, Jeet Kune Do and Filipino Martial Arts practitioner and currently co-hosts the popular Yorkshire-themed podcast Flat Cap Chat.

ANDREW STATON has been involved with the Bruce Lee phenomena since 1974. In the 1980s, he began running the Bruce Lee Collector's Club, which later became The Bruce and Brandon Lee Association.

Staton has worked on many film and TV documentaries and was an associate producer on Bruce Lee Martial Arts Master. He has written hundreds of articles and supplements for the magazines Impact and Martial Arts Illustrated and more recently, wrote the Jun Fan Journal column for the magazine World of Martial Arts.

He currently focuses on the Jun Fan Journal Facebook page and magazine dedicated to Bruce and Brandon Lee news.

CHRIS KENT is widely acknowledged as one of the world's foremost authorities on Jeet Kune Do. With over five decades of in-depth experience, he has gained international recognition for his knowledge and leadership in perpetuating the art, training methods, and philosophy developed by the legendary Bruce Lee.

Chris has authored five top-rated books on Jeet Kune Do including *The Encyclopedia of Jeet Kune Do: A-Z* and *The Jeet Kune Do Guide to Equipment Training*. His recent book, *LIBERATE YOURSELF! – How to Think Like Bruce Lee* details how individuals can apply the philosophical tenets of self-actualisation utilised by Bruce Lee to their own lives. His articles dealing with JKD have appeared in numerous martial art publications, both national and international.

Chris was one of the co-founders of The Bruce Lee Educational Foundation and for five years served as a member of the Board of Directors.

PETER JAGGER is a freelance writer and martial artist from the Midlands.

He has attained the follow grades: Black Belt 1st Dan Tae Kwon Do, Black Belt 1st Dan Wado Ryu Karate, Black Belt 2nd Dan Freestyle Karate, Black Belt 3rd Dan Choi Kwang Do, Black Belt 5th Dan Bushindo Kai, Black Belt 5th Dan WKA, Black Belt 6th Dan Applied Self Defence, Black Belt 6th Dan WBBB, Black Belt 6th Dan WKC, and P4 Krav Maga. He is also graded in other martial arts style and systems.

In 2006, together with Glen Lawrence, he co-founded ASAP Self Defence.

www.ingramcontent.com/pod-product-compliance
Lightning Source LLC
Chambersburg PA
CBHW041315110526
44591CB00022B/2917